Collins
revision guides

InstantRe

CW00734079

GCSE English

Contents

Published by HarperCollins*Publishers* Ltd
77–85 Fulham Palace Road
London W6 8JB

---

www.CollinsEducation.com

On-line support for schools and colleges

British Library Cataloguing in Publication Data
A catalogue record for this publication is available from the British Library

Edited by Steve Attmore
Production by Jack Murphy
Design by Gecko Limited
Printed and bound in China by Imago.

Acknowledgements
The Author and Publishers are grateful to the following for permission to reproduce copyright material:
Penguin Books for *The Go-Between* by L P Hartley, *A Kestrel for a Knave* © Barry Hines, 1968 and *The Kingdom by the Sea* by Paul Theroux; *I'm the King of the Castle* by Susan Hill © Susan Hill, 1970; *Animal Farm* © George Orwell, 1945 by permission of Mark Hamilton as Literary Executor of Estate of the late Sonia Brownell Orwell and Martin Secker & Warburg Ltd; Faber & Faber Ltd for *Lord of the Flies* by William Golding and lines from Ted Hughes' 'Thistles' in *Wodwo*, Seamus Heaney's 'Storm on the Island', 'Digging' and 'The Early Purges' and Simon Armitage's 'I Am Very Bothered'; 'The Darkess Out There' from Penelope Lively's *Pack of Cards and Other Stories, Going Solo* by Roald Dahl and *Under Milk Wood* and 'The Outing: A Story' in *A Dylan Thomas Treasury* are reprinted by permission of David Higham Associates; Random House Publishers for *Salt on the Snow* by Rukshana Smith, *Hobson's Choice* by Harold Brighouse, *Slow Boats to China* by Gavin Young and lines from Maya Angelou's 'Life Doesn't Frighten Me' in *And Still I Rise*; 'Turned' by Charlotte Perkins Gilman (pp 7 and 86) from *The Charlotte Gilman Reader* edited by Anne Lane, published in Great Britain by The Women's Press Ltd, 1985, 34 Great Sutton Street, London EC1V 0DX used by permission of The Women's Press Ltd; Carcanet Press Ltd for lines from Gillian Clarke's 'Sunday', 'Jac Codi Baw' and 'Will Williams (1861–1910)'; lines from 'Poem at Thirty-Nine' (p. 14) are from *Horses Make a Landscape more Beautiful* by Alice Walker, published in Great Britain by The Women's Press Ltd, 1985, 34 Great Sutton Street, London EC1V 0DX, used by permission of David Higham Associates; *A View from the Bridge* by Arthur Miller © 1995, 1957 by Arthur Miller. Reproduced by permission of the author c/o Rogers, Coleridge & White Ltd, 20 Powis Mews, London W11 1JN in association with International Creative Management Inc., 40 West 57th Street, New York, NY10019, USA; from *Boys from the Blackstuff* and *Shop Thy Neighbour* by Alan Bleasdale reproduced by permission of the author; lines from Teresa Hooley's 'A War Film' © Estate of Teresa Hooley; lines from 'Attack' © Siegfried Sassoon by permission of George Sassoon; *Invisible Mass of the Back Row* © Claudette Williams and NATE, 1994, from *Inside Ant's Belly*, edited by Merle Collins and Marva Buchanan, reproduced with permission; verses from W H Auden's 'Stop all the clocks' © 1936 W H Auden, reprinted by permission of Curtis Brown Ltd; lines from Nissim Ezekiel's 'Poverty Poems – 2' in *Collected Poems* and 'Night of the Scorpion' in *Latter Day Psalms* reprinted by permission of Oxford University Press, New Delhi; short story 'There was Once' in the book *Good Bones* by Margaret Atwood, published by Bloomsbury Publishing plc in 1992 is reprinted with permission of the author; lines from 'Even Tho' reproduced with permission of Curtis Brown Ltd, London, on behalf of Grace Nichols © Grace Nichols 1989; *Push Me, Pull Me* by Sandra Chick, first published by The Women's Press Ltd, 1987, 34 Great Sutton Street, London EC1V 0DX, is used by permission of The Women's Press Ltd; *Please Don't Call it Soviet Georgia* by Mary Russell reprinted by permission of Serpent's Tail, London; A M Heath: *The Hidden Land* by Ursula Graham Bower; *Burmese Days* © George Orwell, 1934 by permission of Mark Hamilton as the Literary Executor of the Estate of the late Sonia Brownell Orwell and Martin Secker & Warburg 1995, published by Black Swan, a division of Transworld Publishers Ltd. All rights reserved; *And when did you last see your father?* by Blake Morrison by permission of The Peters Fraser & Dunlop Group Ltd; *Hong Kong* by permission of A P Watt Ltd on behalf of Jan Morris; *Original Sin* © 1994 P D James published by Faber & Faber Ltd and by Penguin. Reproduced by permission of Greene & Heaton Ltd; Sarawak Foundation: *Good Morning and Good Night* by Lady Margaret Brooke.

Photographs/realia
Still/Imageworks (on p. 2); John Cleese/Connie Booth (p. 22); NatWest (p. 49); British Telecommunications plc (p. 54); Rover Group Ltd (p. 2); Haymarket Motoring Publications Ltd *What Car?* May 1998 (p. 59); Health Education Authority (p. 61); BFI Stills/Canal & Image UK (p. 71); Telegraph Colour Library/Larry Bray (p. 115).

Illustrations
Gecko Ltd, John Plumb and Chris Rothero

Every effort has been made to contact the holders of copyright material. If any have been inadvertently overlooked, the Publishers will be pleased to make the necessary arrangements at the first opportunity.

You might also like to visit: www.**fire**and**water**.com

The book lover's website

Get the most out of your
Instant Revision
pocket book

1 **Maximise your revision time.** You can carry this book around with you anywhere. This means you can spend any spare moments dipping into it.

2 **Learn and remember what you need to know.** This book contains all the really important things you need to know for your exam. All the information is set out clearly and concisely, making it easy for you to revise.

3 **Find out what you don't know.** The *Check yourself* questions and *Score chart* help you to see quickly and easily the topics you're good at and those you're not so good at.

What's in this book?

1 *The facts* – just what you need to know

Reading and Writing
- There are sections covering all the important reading and writing topics that you will need in your GCSE English exam.

- The author uses carefully chosen examples from fiction and non-fiction texts to show you how to improve your skills.

Speaking and Listening
- These sections tell you how you can improve your performance.

Exam guidance
- These sections give you hints on how to prepare for your exams and on how to tackle exam questions.

2 *Check yourself* questions – find out how much you know and boost your grade

- Each *Check yourself* is linked to one or more facts page. The numbers after the topic heading in the *Check yourself* tell you which facts page the *Check yourself* is linked to.

- The questions ask you to demonstrate the types of skills you will need to use in the exams. They will show you what you are good at and what you need to improve on.

- The reverse side of each *Check yourself* gives you the answers **plus** tutorial help and guidance to boost your exam grade.

- There are points for each question. The total number of points for each *Check yourself* is always 20. When you check your answers, fill in the score box alongside each answer with the number of points you feel you scored.

3 The *Score chart* – an instant picture of your strengths and weaknesses

- *Score chart (1)* lists all the *Check yourself* pages.

- As you complete each *Check yourself*, record your points on the *Score chart*. This will show you instantly which areas you need to spend more time on.

- *Score chart (2)* is a graph which lets you plot your points against GCSE grades. This will give you a rough idea of how you are doing in each area. Of course, this is only a rough idea because the questions aren't real exam questions!

Use this Instant Revision pocket book on your own – or revise with a friend or relative. See who can get the highest score!

Examiners will expect you to explain how writers create interesting characters and use them to convey ideas and attitudes. There are three basic ways of doing this, although often they will be used in combination.

Character through description

This is the first description of Mrs Kingshaw in *I'm the King of the Castle* by Susan Hill:

> **She was widowed, she was thirty-seven, and she was to become what he had termed an informal housekeeper.**

There is no physical description, so we have no idea at this stage what Mrs Kingshaw looks like. Our interest is gained by making us wonder, for example, what has attracted Mr Hooper to Mrs Kingshaw? What does he mean by 'informal housekeeper'? So the author's technique is one of giving a little information to make us want to read on.

Descriptions may be more detailed. This is Marian in *The Go-Between* by L. P. Hartley:

> Her father's long eyelids drooped over her eyes, leaving under them a glint of blue so deep and liquid that it might have been shining through an unshed tear. Her hair was bright with sunshine, but her face, which was full like her mother's, only pale rose-pink instead of cream, wore a stern brooding look that her small curved nose made almost hawk-like.

You could sketch Marian's appearance from this information, but not Mrs Kingshaw. However, there is a similarity in the descriptions, and it is an important technique which you should comment on when writing about character. This is the **implicit** meaning in the descriptions; that is, what the authors are suggesting about the characters. Marian is obviously beautiful, but words such as 'stern', 'brooding' and 'hawk-like' hint at harsh elements in her character; the lack of information about Mrs Kingshaw makes her seem mysterious and even a little threatening. Susan Hill and L. P. Hartley have got us speculating about their characters – in one case through lack of detail, and in the other through the amount of detail!

READING PROSE FICTION (2)

Character through action

Rather than simply describe them, the author may show us characters doing things. Our reactions to what they do help us decide what kind of people they are. When Billy Casper in *A Kestrel for a Knave* washes his hands after a fight at school, he plays with a soap bubble:

> He tilted his hand and shifted his head to catch the colours from different angles and in different lights, and while he was looking it vanished, leaving him looking at a lathered palm.

What is the author, Barry Hines, telling us? Despite his problems, Billy is a sensitive lad who delights in the natural world around him. On a more basic level, he is not used to having hot water and soap to wash with!

Character through speech

Squealer in *Animal Farm* by George Orwell shows his character through what he says. Here we see his cunning and disregard for the other animals:

> We pigs are brain workers. The whole management and organisation of this farm depend on us. Day and night we are watching over your welfare. It is for your sake that we drink that milk and eat those apples. Do you know what would happen if we pigs failed in our duty? Yes, Jones would come back!

It is **what** he says which shows Squealer's nature. Sometimes it will be how a character says something which is revealing. In *The Darkness Out There* by Penelope Lively, Mrs Rutter shows how little she minds about the death of a German airman (but also her anger at the death of her own husband in the war) by commenting, '*Tit for tat...*'.

Check yourself

Reading prose fiction (1–2)

1 What should you comment on in descriptions of characters? (1)

2 How can a writer use action to reveal character? (1)

3 In what two ways can character be revealed through speech? (2)

4 What do you learn about the character of the boy in this excerpt from William Golding's *Lord of the Flies*? What details help you form your ideas? (6)

> He was a boy of perhaps six years, sturdy and fair, his clothes torn, his face covered with a sticky mess of fruit. His trousers had been lowered for an obvious purpose and had only been pulled back half-way. He jumped off the palm terrace into the sand and his trousers fell about his ankles; he stepped out of them and trotted to the platform.... As he received the reassurance of something purposeful being done he began to look satisfied, and his only clean digit, a pink thumb, slid into his mouth.

5 What do this girl's actions (from *The Darkness Out There* by Penelope Lively) tell you about her character? (4)

> She stopped to pick grass stems out of her sandal; she saw the neat print of the strap-marks against her sunburn, pink-white on brown. Somebody had said she had pretty feet, once: she looked at them clean and plump and neat on the grass.

6 What does this dialogue tell you about the three characters in *Salt on the Snow* by Rukshana Smith? (6)

> 'I saw an ad for a volunteer agency today,' Julie remarked. 'I thought I might find out about it. They're asking for helpers to get old people's shopping.' Dad looked up, his mouth full. 'Do-gooders!' he scoffed. 'Charity work! You know I don't hold with that sort of thing.' 'Don't upset yourself, Jack,' soothed his wife, pouring him a cup of tea.

1 Implicit or suggested meanings (1).

2 By making a character do something which will cause a reaction in the reader (1).

3 Through *how* a character says something (1) and through *what* a character says (1).

4 The boy seems to be adventurous (1) as he has been exploring and finding fruit to eat (1); he is not easily embarrassed (1) as he hadn't pulled his trousers up properly after going to the toilet and steps right out of them when they fall down (1). Despite this, he is obviously a little frightened or lonely (1) as he sucks his thumb (1).

Note how each statement about the boy's character is supported by a detail from the text. You can either put the details into your own words, or you might quote directly from the passage.

5 She likes to be neat and tidy/comfortable (1) as she stops to pick grass stems out of her sandal (1). She may be a little vain (1) because she remembers how someone once complimented her feet and she admires them now (1).

This question requires you to read more between the lines than question 4. However, if you consider carefully what the girl does and thinks, that should give you clues about her character.

6 Julie is kind and helpful (1) as she wants to be a volunteer helper (1); Dad is aggressive and scornful (1) as is shown by his word 'do-gooders' (1) and the author's word 'scoffed' (1); Mum is the peacemaker (1) as we see from the author's word 'soothed'.

Here it is the characters' actual language rather than their actions which gives a hint about their attitudes, but remember to look for other help such as the author's choice of words (here: 'remarked', 'scoffed' and 'soothed') which describes **how** they say something.

TOTAL

Apart from character, the aspect of prose fiction which most influences how you respond to an author's concerns is **setting**. Setting means the ways in which places or objects are used to create *meaning, atmosphere* or *mood*.

Settings which create meaning

Sometimes a description will appear to be literal or neutral if the writer simply wants to establish where something is happening:

> The house, which was called Warings, had been built by the boy's great-grandfather, and so it was not very old. In those days, there had been a large village, and the first Joseph Hooper had owned a good deal of land. Now, the village had shrunk, people had left for the towns and there had been few newcomers, few new buildings. Derne had become like an old busy port which has been deserted by the sea.

That extract from *I'm the King of the Castle* gives background information in a straightforward way. Even so, a skilful writer like Susan Hill cannot avoid suggesting in the final sentence that the village has not merely shrunk in size, but has actually been rejected by people – what is wrong with this place, the reader might wonder.

Descriptions of places are often used to create meaning. In this passage from *Lord of the Flies*, the sea is made to seem monstrous and threatening:

> ...it seemed like the breathing of some stupendous creature. Slowly the waters sank among the rocks, revealing pink tables of granite, strange growths of coral, polyp, and weed. Down, down, the waters went, whispering like the wind among the heads of the forest. There was one flat rock there, spread like a table, and the waters sucking down on the four weedy sides made them seem like cliffs. Then the sleeping leviathan breathed out – the waters rose, the weed streamed, and the water boiled over the table rock with a roar.

Words such as 'breathing', 'creature', 'growths', 'whispering', 'heads', 'sucking' and 'breathed' give the sea human qualities. These convey both the threat of the environment and the fear of the boy watching it. So, as well as helping to establish William Golding's theme of savagery, the passage also tells us about Ralph's feelings.

Settings which create mood or atmosphere

Setting can thus be used to illustrate a character's mood, or to set the tone of a story. The narrator in Dylan Thomas's *The Outing* tells us:

> The charabanc pulled up outside the Mountain Sheep, a small, unhappy public house with a thatched roof like a wig with ringworm …

Here the mix of comedy and disappointment reflects both the narrator's feelings and the atmosphere of the story.

Barry Hines begins *A Kestrel for a Knave* with this paragraph:

> There were no curtains up. The window was a hard edged block the colour of the night sky. Inside the bedroom the darkness was of a gritty texture. The wardrobe and the bed were blurred shapes in the darkness. Silence.

This sets the mood for the whole story, which is indeed 'hard' and 'gritty'. This 'silence' is not peaceful, but threatening, with the 'blurred shapes' lurking in the 'darkness'.

When you consider setting, look for meaning both in **what** is described and **how** it is described; think about what these choices tell you about characters in the story or about the actual themes and ideas of the story. Look especially at the words used, and any images – such as William Golding's comparison of the sea to a monster or Dylan Thomas's comparison of the thatch to a rotten wig.

Reading prose fiction (3–4)

1 How does the author convey Rashmi's mood through the setting of this extract from *Salt on the Snow*? (4)

> ...she washed up, staring out of the window. Everything was grey. The flats opposite were coated in greyish pebbledash, the sky was grey, grey-faced people in grey coats hurried by, their eyes downcast on the grey paths. 'Back home,' she thought, 'houses are painted green and yellow with contrasting patterns around the doors.'

2 What do these descriptions of two different settings, both from near the start of *Turned*, suggest about the theme of Charlotte Perkins Gilman's story? (4)

> In her soft-carpeted, thick-curtained, richly-furnished chamber, Mrs Marroner lay sobbing on the wide, soft bed.
>
> In her uncarpeted, thin-curtained, poorly-furnished chamber on the top floor, Gerta Petersen lay sobbing on the narrow, hard bed.

3 How does this extract from *I'm the King of the Castle* **(a)** establish a particular atmosphere (10) and **(b)** suggest to you the mood of the two boys, Kingshaw and Hooper? (2)

> There was a sudden screeching cry, and a great flapping of wings, like wooden clappers. Kingshaw looked up. Two jays came flying straight through the wood, their wings whirring on the air. When they had gone, it went very still again at once, and it seemed darker, too. Then, a faint breeze came through the wood towards them, and passed, just stirring the warm air. Silence again. A blackbird began to sing, a loud, bright, warning song. Hooper looked up in alarm. From somewhere, far away, came the first rumble of thunder...

1   Rashmi is depressed (1) and homesick (1). This is emphasised
    by the repetition of the word 'grey' (1) and how she contrasts
    this in her mind with the colourfulness of her native country (1).
    This is a fairly obvious example of a writer using contrasting
    colours to suggest different feelings or attitudes. Always be on
    the look out for more subtle uses of colour to reinforce the
    theme or message of a piece of writing: such details are
    seldom there by chance – writers choose words for reasons!

2   Both passages describe similar details of setting, but in one
    case they are expensive (1) and in the other cheap (1). This
    suggests that one theme of the story may be differences in
    social class (1) but that people experience the same emotions
    no matter what class they belong to (1).
    Again, this is a fairly obvious example of a technique. Here,
    the author is repeating the structure of a description, but
    changing aspects to contrast characters' lifestyles. In this
    story, the two descriptions occur within a few lines of each
    other, but be prepared to recognise this technique even if the
    contrasts are several chapters, or hundreds of pages, apart.

3 **(a)**   The atmosphere is threatening (1) and this is
            emphasised by words such as 'screeching' (1), 'cry' (1),
            'warning' (1) and 'alarm' (1). This atmosphere is
            strengthened by the shock the boys get from the two
            jays (1), from the changes in the movement of the air (1),
            the increasing darkness (1), the silence broken by the
            blackbird's warning (1) and the sudden rumble of
            thunder (1).
   (b)   The boys are probably both a little frightened (1) –
            Hooper certainly shows alarm (1).
    This passage is full of symbols which convey atmosphere and
    suggest mood. Notice how some of this comes through
    individual words and some through general description.

TOTAL

Sound effects

When you read a poem, what does it sound like? Do the sounds have anything to do with its subject matter? If you speak a poem out loud, how much effort does it take to pronounce the words? Do the sounds of the words, and the effort it takes to make them, help you share the poet's feelings or sense the atmosphere the poet is trying to create?

When Wilfred Owen, a soldier-poet of the First World War, writes about '*the merciless iced east winds that knive us*', the sounds (that is, all the *c*s, *s*s and *i*s) make you feel as though you are experiencing the biting cold, and sharing his despair.

Owen's line shows examples of both **alliteration** (when the same sound is repeated, for example the *c*s, *s*s and *i*s) and of **onomatopoeia** (when the sound of a word imitates the sound of what it describes). 'Wind' is an onomatopoeic word, as you make a blowing sound when you pronounce it. So is 'knive', as the sound of the word is sharp and violent, just like the effect of the cold wind it describes.

Poets often use alliteration and onomatopoeia together. Their choice of words may also be influenced by the physical effort the reader needs to make when speaking them out loud. In the Owen extract, 'knive' ends with a rasping *v* sound, and the *c*s and *s*s in the other words are very forceful too as you need to force air between your teeth to pronounce them.

In complete contrast, Lord Alfred Tennyson uses gentle, soothing sounds in the following lines from his poem *In Memoriam*. These require little effort on the speaker's part and so reinforce the alliteration and onomatopoeia. They create the effect of a hot, drowsy summer afternoon.

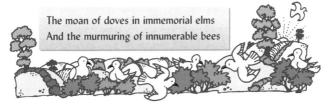

> The moan of doves in immemorial elms
> And the murmuring of innumerable bees

Imagery

Poets often use original **imagery** to convey their meaning. The image may relate an object, place or emotion to something with which you are familiar, so that you can share the poet's feelings. When Gillian Clarke writes '*Like peaty water sun slowly fills the long brown room*' she is using a **simile**, where the word 'like' makes a direct comparison of one thing (sunlight) to something else (peaty water). In this example, the simile helps you picture a room which remains rather gloomy and mysterious despite the brightness which comes into it. It allows you to share the feelings of apprehension which the poem describes.

Imagery may be used to shock you into seeing something in a different way, if the poet compares the familiar or comfortable with something frightening or disturbing. For example, to Ted Hughes 'thistles'

> are like pale hair and the gutturals of dialects.
> Every one manages a plume of blood.

Here there is a simile in the first sentence. The reference to 'a plume of blood' is a **metaphor** – there isn't really blood on the thistles, just a purply-red colouring on their tips, but the image suggests the violence Ted Hughes associates with thistles.

Hughes also uses the technique known as **personification**, when objects or places are made to seem alive by the words used to describe them. In the final lines of Hughes' poem, personification is combined with metaphor and simile to reinforce the threat he sees in thistles:

> Then they grow grey like men.
> Mown down, it is a feud. Their sons appear,
> Stiff with weapons, fighting back over the
>   same ground.

Reading poetry (1–2)

1 (a) Identify the alliteration in these lines from Seamus Heaney's *Storm on the Island* (1).

(b) What effect does it have on the reader (2), and **(c)** why? (1)

> when it begins, the flung spray hits
> The very window, spits like a tame cat
> Turned savage.

2 (a) How is onomatopoeia used in the following lines by Gillian Clarke (3), and **(b)** what effect does it have on the reader? (2)

> War planes have been at it all day long
> shaking the world, strung air
> humming like pianos when children bang the keys.

3 Explain simile, metaphor and personification (3).

4 The following lines are from a poem by Seamus Heaney in which he describes the death of his four-year-old brother.

(a) Identify a simile and a metaphor (2).

(b) Explain the meaning of each (2).

(c) What effect do they have on the reader (2)?

> Wearing a poppy bruise on his left temple,
> He lay in the four-foot box as in his cot.

5 (a) How is personification used in this extract from a war poem by Wilfred Owen (1), and **(b)** to what effect? (1)

> Dawn massing in the east her melancholy army
> Attacks once more in ranks on shivering ranks of gray.

1 (a) The letter *s* is used several times (1).
   (b) This reinforces the meaning of the lines (1), which are describing the onset of a storm (1).
   (c) The sound of the letter is produced by forcing air between the teeth (1).

2 (a) The onomatopoeic words are 'shaking' (1), 'humming' (1) and 'bang' (1).
   (b) 'Shaking' and 'bang' relate to the mention of war planes and reinforce the sense of violence and/or fear (1), while 'humming' creates a feeling of tension (1).

You need to hear a poem inside your mind to judge the impact of sound effects. Think also about the physical effort needed to produce certain sounds or to pronounce words.

3 A simile compares one thing with something else, using words such as 'like' or 'as' (1). A metaphor describes something directly as though it were something else (1). Personification is making an inanimate object seem human, or alive (1).

4 (a) 'A poppy bruise' is a metaphor (1); 'As in his cot' is a simile (1).
   (b) The metaphor conveys the colour, shape and size of the bruise (1); the simile suggests sleep and/or peacefulness (1).
   (c) The metaphor saddens the reader by reinforcing the theme of death through the association of the poppy with Remembrance Day (1); the simile emphasises the fact that the body is that of a young child and makes the reader feel a sense of waste (1).

Notice how an image may require you to look beyond the immediate text to gain the author's full meaning, as in this metaphor which refers to a tradition of remembrance.

5 (a) The break of day is compared to an enemy attack (1).
   (b) This makes it seem that even the forces of nature have a personal grudge against the soldiers (1).

TOTAL

Purpose, tone and attitude

When you respond to a poem, you need to think – what is it about and why was it written? Does it make you see situations in a new light or understand feelings in greater depth? When Gillian Clarke describes her car, left near a building which was being demolished, in her poem *Jac Codi Baw* as

> splattered with the stone's blood, smoky with ghosts.

her **purpose** is to help us reflect on how much is actually being destroyed.

Tone refers to the way in which the poet addresses you. It may be to question you or challenge your thinking, as when George Herbert writes in *Jordan*:

> Who says that fictions only and false hair
> Become a verse?

Or the tone may be quite matter-of-fact. Nissim Ezekiel begins the poem *Night of the Scorpion*:

> I remember the night my mother
> was stung by a scorpion.

Attitude means the poet's viewpoint: is the 'I' in the poem the poet him or herself, or is the writing ironically putting forward ideas the poet does not hold? In the lines by Gillian Clarke above, it seems quite clear that she is expressing her own attitude of sadness. But to decide if Simon Armitage is being honest in his poem which begins

> I am very bothered when I think
> of the bad things I have done in my life.

you would need to consider the whole poem very carefully.

Form

The **form** of a poem can also affect your response to it. Regular rhyme and rhythm may often create a happy, light-hearted mood and convey simple ideas – or the poet may use the form ironically to contrast with, and emphasise, a sombre message. This is what William Blake does in his poem *London*:

> But most thro' midnight streets I hear
> How the youthful harlot's curse
> Blasts the new-born infant's tear,
> And blights with plagues the marriage hearse.

Poems which have an irregular rhythm and little, or no, rhyme can seem more like a conversation. It may feel as though the poet is talking directly to you, especially if the language is blunt and everyday rather than formal. This is Seamus Heaney in his poem *The Early Purges*:

> I was six when I first saw kittens drown.
> Dan Taggart pitched them, 'the scraggy wee shits',
> Into a bucket

Sometimes the form of a poem can imitate its meaning, as in the opening of this poem by Alice Walker, *Poem at Thirty-Nine*, where the shortening lines seem to illustrate her tired father running out of energy:

> How I miss my father.
> I wish he had not been
> so tired
> when I was
> born.

Always try to comment on the form of a poem: it is chosen for a purpose by the poet, as carefully as the ideas, words and images are chosen.

Reading poetry (3–4)

1 How would you define purpose, tone and attitude in a poem? (3)

2 (a) What do you think was William Blake's purpose in writing the following poem? (3)

(b) What is the tone of the poem, and what attitudes does it display? (3)

> O Rose, thou art sick!
> The invisible worm,
> That flies in the night,
> In the howling storm,
>
> Has found out thy bed
> Of crimson joy,
> And his dark secret love
> Does thy life destroy.

3 What could you write about if you were asked to discuss the form of a poem? (5)

4 (a) What are the features of the form in which these lines (by Maya Angelou) are written? (4)

(b) How effectively does the form suit the poet's purpose? (2)

> I go boo
> Make them shoo
> I make fun
> Way them run
> I won't cry
> So they fly
> I just smile
> They go wild
> Life doesn't frighten me at all.

1 Purpose is why the poem has been written – what the poet wants you to think about (1). Tone is the way in which the poet addresses you (1). Attitude is the point of view expressed (1).

2 (a) Blake's purpose is to remind readers that even beautiful objects like a rose do not last for ever (1) and can be spoilt or destroyed by unseen enemies (1); in other words, you need to be on the look out for trouble or danger all the time (1).

(b) The tone is direct (1) and challenging (1); Blake's attitude is one of concern (1).

The purpose of a poem may be 'between the lines', as in this case – it is not really about a rose at all. When answering a question like this, look at the language and imagery used to help you suggest meanings. There are no right or wrong answers, but some will be more sensible than others. So pay close attention to tone when describing attitude and purpose.

3 You could describe the patterns of rhythm (1) and rhyme (1) in the poem, and whether the language is formal or informal (1). You could also describe any particular verse patterns (1). You should remember to comment on the effects all these features have on you (1).

Whenever you are responding to poetry you must pay constant attention to the **language** of the poem. This may be done when you are considering sound effects and imagery, as well as when you are looking at the structure of the poem or at its tone, attitudes and purpose – all of these aspects are affected by the poet's choice of words.

4 (a) The extract is made up of four pairs of rhyming lines (1) and a longer line at the end which does not rhyme (1). The language is colloquial or everyday (1). The rhythm is simple and regular until the last line (1).

(b) The effect is of a cheerful and/or confident poet (1), and the changed rhythm of the last line emphasises it as the message of the poem (1).

TOTAL

Plays are written to be performed. Respond to them as a member
of an audience – what effect would situations, characters, language
have on you?

- How would the staging of each scene (the set, costumes, props)
  affect an audience's response?
- What relationships do the characters have with each other?
  How is this signalled to the audience?
- What is the play really about? In other words, what is the author's
  purpose or 'message'? How is this made clear to the audience?

Interpreting character and meaning

Responding to the author's use of language is crucial. This may be
within stage directions, for example when the grumpy teacher in Willy
Russell's *Our Day Out* replies to a cheerful colleague's greeting:
'Morning'.

Even a simple piece of punctuation can help. When Basil Fawlty says
'Sorry?' to a guest, the question mark shows that he is either in one of
his usual states of confusion or challenging aggressively. He is not
being apologetic – that would be out of character.

Authors may give detailed directions and descriptions, so that you
react in a way which suits their purpose. When we first see Eliza in
Shaw's *Pygmalion*, the script says:

> *She is not at all a romantic figure. She is perhaps eighteen,*
> *perhaps twenty, hardly older. She wears a little sailor hat of*
> *black straw that has long been exposed to the dust and soot*
> *of London and has seldom, if ever, been brushed ...*

and so on, for another ten lines. What this kind of scripting tells us is
that the playwright is particularly concerned that the audience sees
the characters and receives the play's 'message' exactly as s/he
imagined them.

Dramatic devices

Dramatists use various devices to shape the audience's reactions. In *A View from the Bridge*, Arthur Miller uses Alfieri not only as a character in the play, but also as a commentator to step out of the action and talk directly to us:

> It was at this time that he first came to me. I had represented his father in an accident case some years before, and I was acquainted with the family in a casual way. I remember him now as he walked through my doorway –

at which point the action resumes with that meeting, enabling Miller to switch timescales and have a mouthpiece for his message at the same time.

Dramatic irony – that is, when you know more than the characters on stage – can create striking effects. You may feel an almost physical involvement with the action – at its most obvious level, this occurs in pantomime when a whole audience will shout out to a character on stage, 'Behind you!'

Radio, television and film scripts

A radio play depends almost entirely on the power and originality of its language. So be prepared to comment on how the author captures your imagination through the choice of words, and how sound effects and silences add to the drama.

Comment on how television and film may use a range of special effects – such as multiple screens, flashbacks, non-fiction inserts, long shots and close-ups – to affect your response to characters and themes. In a visual medium, language may seem less important – you may see characters in situations where no words are spoken. You need to consider whether the medium helps or hinders the author's purpose, and whether the author has exploited fully the technical possibilities offered by the medium.

Reading drama (1–2)

1 In this extract from *Hobson's Choice* by Harold Brighouse, what do you learn about the characters of Maggie (2) and Albert (2), and how is this done? (2)

> ALBERT ... I'll just have a pair of bootlaces, please.
>
> MAGGIE What size do you take in boots?
>
> ALBERT Eights. I've got small feet. *[He simpers, then perceives that Maggie is by no means smiling.]* Does that matter to the laces?
>
> MAGGIE *[putting mat in front of armchair]* It matters to the boots. *[She pushes him slightly.]* Sit down, Mr Prosser.

2 Read this extract from *Under Milk Wood* by Dylan Thomas:

> It is spring, moonless night in the small town, starless and bible-black, the cobblestreets silent and the hunched, courters'-and-rabbits' wood limping invisible down to the sloeblack, slow, black, crowblack, fishingboat-bobbing sea.

(a) Explain three ways in which the author uses words imaginatively, giving examples from the text (6).

(b) Give two reasons why this extract would work well as a radio script (2).

3 Read this extract from Alan Bleasdale's television series, *Boys from the Blackstuff*:

> YOSSER You're Graeme Souness. Aren't you?
>
> SOUNESS Yes.
>
> YOSSER You're famous.
>
> SOUNESS Well ...
>
> YOSSER I'm Yosser Hughes.
> *[As if this explains everything]*
>
> SOUNESS Pleased to meet you.
>
> *[YOSSER leans towards him, as if about to disclose a secret.]*
>
> YOSSER You look like me ...
>
> SOUNESS Oh aye.
>
> YOSSER Magnum as well.
>
> SOUNESS Pardon?
>
> YOSSER Magnum. A detective. He used to be on the television. An American.

(a) How is the medium of television important to this scene (2)?

(b) What do you learn about Yosser's character from the extract (4)?

1 Maggie is assertive/bossy (1) and businesslike/stands no nonsense (1). Albert is vain/stuck-up (1) and lacking common sense (1). This is shown both in what each character says (1) and in the stage directions (1).

Note how Maggie fails to respond to Albert's feeble attempt at humour, and how she 'helps' him into the chair.

2 (a) The author uses alliteration on the letter *s* (1) to create the sound effect of the sea (1); he uses assonance/rhyme in sloeblack, slow, black (1) to create the effect of the movement of waves (1); he uses an invented compound word 'fishingboat-bobbing' (1) to create both a visual picture and the rhythmic effect of the boats on the sea (1).

(b) The extract would work well as a radio script because the large number of descriptive words used conjure up a strong visual image (1) and the sound of the words is also appropriate to their meaning (1).

No sound effects or music are used here, but remember to consider the contribution they can make to radio drama, where appropriate.

3 (a) The medium of television is important to this scene because it allows the use of a real person, Graeme Souness (1); it also allows close-ups to show Yosser leaning towards him (1).

(b) We learn that Yosser is someone without any sense of embarrassment (1) from the way he introduces himself to a famous footballer (1). He also appears slightly obsessive or detached from reality (1) from his comments about his resemblance to both Souness and a television star (1).

It would be very difficult to perform a scene like this on stage, as a star footballer would have to be available for every performance alongside the actors! The use of close-ups also allows actors to use a subtle range of facial expression, or slight body movements, which would go unnoticed in a theatre.

TOTAL

Writing which conveys **factual information** must make its meaning clear. It must not cause doubts or uncertainty in the reader's mind. If you have to read this kind of text twice, it has failed in its purpose. The language of such texts avoids opinion, emotion and implication; the writer's attitudes or personality are not important. Language is used here literally.

Literary texts are different: they have succeeded if you can find alternative meanings when you read them. The language of a well-written literary text is full of qualities such as the author's mood, ideas and values.

In literal language, a spade is a spade and a pen is a pen. Literary language, by using images and allusions (reference to a person, event or story), can make us see how one might be like the other. Read this extract from the poem *Digging* by Seamus Heaney:

> Between my finger and my thumb
> The squat pen rests.
> I'll dig with it.

Seamus Heaney realises that his tool – the pen – is like his father's tool which was a spade. Neither tool is better than the other, and both men create worthwhile things with them.

Metaphor and symbolism

Remember the power of the imagery from William Golding's *Lord of the Flies*:

> ...it seemed like the breathing of some stupendous creature... Then the sleeping leviathan breathed out – the waters rose, the weed streamed, and the water boiled over the table rock with a roar.

Certain words give animal qualities to the sea. They convey the fear of the boy watching it. In the extract from *Thistles* by Ted Hughes (see page 10) we also saw how thistles could be symbolised as threatening in a human way through personification and imagery.

Irony

The meaning of literary texts is often conveyed through the way the reader understands a situation better than the characters involved in it. For example, in Barry Hines' *A Kestrel for a Knave*, Mr Gryce the Headteacher sees nothing odd in singing a hymn about God's love at an assembly mostly taken up by shouting at the pupils (and sometimes the staff). Irony may also be very bitter. An example is this extract from Siegfried Sassoon's poem:

> Does it matter? Losing your sight?
> There's such splendid work for the blind:
> And people will always be kind.

Irony can also be subtle. In Penelope Lively's *The Darkness Out There*, it is only at the end of the story that the reader realises how inappropriate this early, gentle description of Mrs Rutter is:

> ...the old woman was back in the armchair, a composite chintzy mass from which cushions oozed and her voice flowed softly on.

Dramatic irony is a common device in plays or sitcoms: you, the audience, know more than the characters on stage and so can be horrified or amused by what they say. In *Fawlty Towers* the audience is already cringing when Basil asks a guest 'And how is that lovely daughter of yours?' long before Sybil quietly reminds him: 'Dead'.

Reading beneath the surface (1–2)

1 What three things do we learn about Sandra in this extract from Penelope Lively's *The Darkness Out There*? Identify a textual clue to support each suggestion. (6)

> She put her sandal back on. She walked through the thicker grass by the hedge and felt it drag at her legs and thought of swimming in warm seas. She put her hand on the top of her head and her hair was hot from the sun, a dry burning cap. One day, this year, next year, sometime, she would go to places like on travel brochures and run into a blue sea. She would fall in love and she would get a good job and she would have one of those new Singers that do zig-zag stitch and make an embroidered silk coat.

2 A mother has seen the horrors of war at the cinema. Later that day she is bathing her baby son. Explain the irony in these lines from Teresa Hooley's *A War Film* (2):

> How should he know
> Why I kissed and kissed and kissed him,
>   crooning his name?
> He thought that I was daft.
> He thought it was a game
> And laughed, and laughed.

3 What is the irony in this situation? (3) It is from *Hobson's Choice* by Harold Brighouse.

HOBSON	I'm going out, Maggie.
MAGGIE	Dinner's at one, remember.
HOBSON	Dinner will be when I come in for it. I'm master here.
MAGGIE	Yes, father. One o'clock.

4 Identify details in the following lines from Dylan Thomas's *The Outing: A Story* which suggest the landlord's different qualities (9):

> The landlord stood at the door to welcome us, simpering like a wolf. He was a long, lean, black-fanged man with a greased love-curl and pouncing eyes. 'What a beautiful August day!' he said, and touched his love-curl with a claw.

1 Sandra is a dreamer (1), suggested by either her thoughts about swimming or falling in love (1). She is probably from a not-very-wealthy family (1) as she can only dream about having expensive holidays or fancy sewing machines (1). She is ambitious (1) as she wants to have a good job/get married/make expensive clothes (1).

Descriptions of characters' thoughts often tell you something about their background and character as well as their hopes and aspirations.

2 The baby laughs, thinking the kissing is a game (1), but the mother remembers the film she has seen and is afraid that he may suffer in the future (1).

3 The irony is that Maggie has the last word (1) despite Hobson saying that he is master in his own home (1). We can presume from these lines that Maggie has the upper hand and Hobson is, in fact, the weaker of the two (1).

Irony can be easy to recognise but difficult to explain. Try to identify what is happening and why, and where any misunderstanding or contradiction occurs.

4 The landlord is a frightening (1) but fascinating (1) man. He is made to seem frightening by words such as 'black-fanged', 'greased', 'pouncing', 'claw' and 'wolf' (5). His attraction is conveyed by 'simpering' and 'love-curl' (2).

TOTAL

One way to show understanding of how texts achieve their effects is to compare how writers tackle a similar theme, idea or situation. You need to think about:

- the language and structure of the texts
- the authors' feelings, values and attitudes
- and what their purposes for writing may have been.

Comparing poems

Look at the ending of Rupert Brooke's *Peace*:

> Nothing to shake the laughing heart's long peace there
> But only agony, and that has ending;
> And the worst friend and enemy is but Death.

Compare this with the ending of Siegfried Sassoon's *Attack*:

> They leave their trenches, going over the top,
> While time ticks blank and busy on their wrists,
> And hope, with furtive eyes and grappling fists,
> Flounders in mud. O Jesus, make it stop!

Both describe death in battle. To Brooke – writing at the start of the First World War – it is something glorious, patriotic, almost without consequence. To Sassoon – writing with several years' experience of the trenches – it is terrifying. Brooke's language is stately and 'poetic'; Sassoon, although he uses the same technique of personification, writes in plain, urgent language. He uses rhythms which reflect meaning (second line) and he uses stop–start phrases and harsh sounds (third and fourth lines). When comparing texts it is a good idea to point out similarities as well as differences. This is often how varying attitudes and values become clear.

Comparing prose

You will sometimes need to compare the presentation of characters. The author's technique may leave you to form your own opinion. Read the extract overleaf from *The Darkness Out There* by Penelope Lively.

> The girl blushed. She looked at the floor, at her own feet,
> neat and slim and brown. She touched, secretly, the soft
> skin of her thigh; she felt her breasts poke up and out at
> the thin stuff of her top; she licked the inside of her teeth,
> that had only the one filling, a speck like a pin-head.

Sandra is a complex character: still childlike, but becoming a young
adult; likeable, but a little vain. The author stresses this complexity by
making you do the work. Sometimes an author needs to move the
story along and introduce you quickly to the main aspects of a
character. Description may then be more obvious – as Claudette
Williams shows in *Invisible Mass of the Back Row*:

> He is big, sturdy and beautifully dark, with a baby moustache. He
> is handsomely dressed in his Dashiki suit. There is a kindness about
> this man that is not usually found among teachers.

Sometimes a character or situation changes within a text. You may be
asked to describe and explain this process by comparing one part of
the text with another. Look at how the teenagers in Penelope Lively's
The Darkness Out There think of Mrs Rutter at the start of the story:

> ...old Mrs Rutter with her wonky leg would be ever so pleased to
> see them because they were really sweet, lots of the old people.

But after they discover the secret of her past, Kerry says about her:

> 'It makes you want to throw up ... someone like that.'

You might explain this change by quoting and explaining the last lines of
the story, seen through the thoughts of Sandra:

> She walked behind him, through a world grown unreliable,
> in which flowers sparkle and birds sing but everything is
> not as it appears, oh no.

Comparing texts (1–2)

Compare the following extracts. Refer to details in each text and comment on detailed similarities and differences in:

(a) theme (3)
(b) attitude (2)
(c) language (8)
(d) structure (7)

Even Tho

Come
leh we hug up
and brace-up
and sweet one another up

But then
leh we break free
yes, leh we break free

And keep to de motion
of we own person/ality

Grace Nichols

Stop all the clocks

He was my North, my South, my East and West,
My working week and my Sunday rest,
My noon, my midnight, my talk, my song;
I thought that love would last forever; I was wrong.

The stars are not wanted now: put out every one;
Pack up the moon and dismantle the sun;
Pour away the ocean and sweep up the wood.
For nothing now can ever come to any good.

W. H. Auden

(a) Both extracts are about love (1), but the first is about lovers who are still together (1) while in the second they have parted (1).

(b) The poets' attitudes differ. The first thinks that lovers should keep their individuality (1) while in the second the poet believes in each being everything to the other (1).

(c) The language of the first extract is in a dialect (1); for example, 'leh we' which would be 'let us' in standard English (1). It is also informal (1); for example the use of 'yes' (1), which makes it sound as though the poet is talking directly to the reader (1). In the second extract, the poet refers to universal objects (1); for example, the stars, the sun and the moon/the points of the compass (1) to show how important his love was to him in his life (1).

(d) The structure of the first extract is free and informal (1), with irregular line-lengths (1) and verse-lengths (1). This reinforces the informality of the language (1). The second extract is in a traditional rhyming couplet format (1) which makes it easy to read (1) and memorable in a song-like way (1).
This should be quite straightforward, as there is a clear contrast between the language and structure of the texts despite the similarity in theme. Note the need to give precise examples to illustrate the points you make.

In an examination, you would probably also be asked to say which text you preferred, and why. This will be a matter of personal response, but it should be based on some of the features commented upon here – for example, do you prefer happy/sad texts, traditional rhyming verse or free form poetry?

TOTAL

Place and time

You may be asked to show your understanding of the relationship of texts to the place and time in which they were written and how that affects their meaning. It may be just a single word which suggests a non-British setting, as in *Poverty Poems – 2* by Nissim Ezekiel:

> I lifted up my eyes
> Near the railway station
> And saw a leper standing
> Against a poster-ridden wall.

Here, the word 'leper' alerts us to the likelihood of a foreign setting. It may be a description of behaviour or beliefs which you can identify as indicating a different social and cultural setting. This extract describes the behaviour of villagers after a neighbour has been bitten by a scorpion:

> The peasants came like swarms of flies
> and buzzed the name of God a hundred times
> to paralyse the Evil One.
> With candles and with lanterns
> throwing giant scorpion shadows
> on the mud-baked walls
> they searched for him…

The worries, ideas and values described in texts are often the same, irrespective of the cultural or social setting. You should therefore look not only for what is distinctive in such texts, but also for what is familiar or universal. Look for how the distinctiveness of the setting makes for originality. In the lines above, from Nissim Ezekiel's *Night of the Scorpion*, the neighbours show the fear and concern you would expect in any society. However, details – such as the candles and lanterns and the actions of the villagers – locate the event firmly within its own culture. This is reinforced by the imagery used, 'swarms of flies' being a particularly appropriate metaphor in the circumstances.

SETTINGS (2)

Cultural, social and historical settings

Social and **cultural** settings may even be imaginary, for example in science-fiction stories. In *Examination Day*, by Henry Slesar, twelve-year-old children are tested and 'eliminated' if they are too intelligent for the needs of their society. So this is the choice facing Dickie's parents at the end of the story:

> 'You may specify by telephone,' the voice droned on, 'whether you wish his body interred by the Government or would you prefer a private burial place? The fee for Government burial is ten dollars.'

The **historical** setting of texts may be shown by the ideas or actions described, but is often most obvious through the language. For example, in this ballad the vocabulary makes it

> As I was walking all alane
> I heard twa corbies making a mane;
> The tane unto the t'other did say
> 'Where sall we gang and dine to-day?'

clear that this is a Scottish poem from an earlier century. The harshness of the vocabulary suits the theme and mood exactly.

Dramatic effect

For dramatic effect, a story or poem may sometimes turn cultural, social and historical expectations on their head. Margaret Atwood, for example, uses a traditional story to create humour out of modern attitudes in *There was Once*:

> – There was once a poor girl, as beautiful as she was good, who lived with her wicked stepmother in a house in the forest.
> – Forest? *Forest* is passe, I mean I've had it with all this wilderness stuff. It's not a right image of our society, today. Let's have some *urban* for a change.

When commenting on these aspects of a text, remember that you must comment on the effects achieved by the social, cultural or historical dimension – shock, amusement, fascination with the unknown, etc.

Settings (1–2)

1 (a) In this extract, from *Even Tho* by Grace Nichols, what are the distinctive social/cultural aspects? (4)

(b) What effects do they achieve? (1)

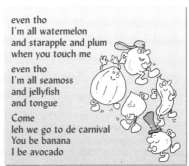

even tho
I'm all watermelon
and starapple and plum
when you touch me

even tho
I'm all seamoss
and jellyfish
and tongue

Come
leh we go to de carnival
You be banana
I be avocado

2 (a) What would you comment on as significant cultural, social and historical details in these verses from William Blake's poem *London*? (8)

(b) What atmosphere do they create? (2)

How the chimney-sweeper's cry
Every blackening church appals;
And the hapless soldier's sigh
Runs in blood down palace walls.

But most thro' midnight streets I hear
How the youthful harlot's curse
Blasts the new-born infant's tear,
And blights with plagues the marriage-hearse.

3 (a) What details in this extract convey a particular sense of culture? (4)

(b) What effect do they achieve? (1)

The boxes are unwrapped. Our senses are assaulted by saltfish fritters, fried dumplings, red herring, cornmeal pudding, sweet potato pudding, oranges, plums, mangoes or sugar-cane, snowball and sky-juice. Smells mingle and whirl, creating a comfortable oasis under the gigantic cotton tree.

1 (a) Social/cultural aspects are in the language (e.g. 'leh we' (1), 'de' (1), and in references to 'starapple' (1) and 'seamoss' (1)).

(b) The effects achieved are that the poem appeals to the senses/is sensuous (1).

2 (a) There are clear references to an earlier age in 'chimney-sweeper' (1). These would have been young children (1). 'Blackening' (1) refers to pollution (1), 'hapless soldiers' (1) refers to warfare (1) and 'youthful harlot' (1) refers to child prostitution (1).

(b) The effects are that the details establish an atmosphere of misery (1), social injustice (1).

Commenting on social and historical features of texts may require some knowledge of the writer's lifetime, but remember this is only background information. In an English examination your main task is to comment on a writer's techniques and effects.

3 (a) The sense of a different culture is established by references to food (1 + 2 for any appropriate examples) and the 'cotton tree' (1).

(b) The effect is one of excitement/enjoyment (1).

TOTAL

In your examination you need to show that you can use technical words which describe how writers make language work for them and achieve their desired effects. Examples of such terms are **alliteration**, **onomatopoeia**, **simile**, **metaphor** and **personification**. (Check back to pages 9–16 if you are unsure of the meanings of any of these words.)

Simply using these words, even knowing the meaning of them, is not enough. To gain high marks in your examination you must be able to explain how any technique works in a particular text. So, for example, in these lines from William Golding's *Lord of the Flies* you would comment how the alliteration and onomatopoeia (particularly the *s* and *sh* sounds) imitate the noise of the sea which they describe. They create a vivid picture in the reader's mind:

> Now the sea would suck down, making cascades and waterfalls of retreating water, would sink past the rocks and plaster down the seaweed like shining hair: then, pausing, gather and rise with a roar, irresistibly swelling over point and outcrop, climbing the little-cliff, sending at last an arm of surf up a gully to end a yard or so from him in fingers of spray.

Similarly, in *Portrait of a Machine* the poet, Louis Untermeyer, does not state directly that the machine is alive. However the words he uses (such as 'nudity', 'monster', 'purring', 'muscles', 'sure-fingered' and 'flank') make the reader think of the machine as some kind of living creature:

> What nudity as beautiful as this
> Obedient monster purring at its toil;
> Those naked iron muscles dripping oil
> And the sure-fingered rods that never miss?
> This long and shining flank of metal is
> Magic that greasy labour cannot spoil

The writer's purpose here is to make you think about the nature of machines. Are they beautiful, or threatening? How much in control of them are we?

SECSI

This is a useful acronym to help you to write about the effects achieved by the language and devices used by writers of fiction texts. Suppose you were responding to these lines from Wilfred Owen's *Dulce et Decorum Est*:

> If you could hear, at every jolt, the blood
> Come gargling from the froth-corrupted lungs,
> Obscene as cancer, bitter as the cud
> Of vile, incurable sores on innocent tongues, –

You might structure your comments the SECSI way:

- **S**tatement – Wilfred Owen wants to shock his readers by revealing the true horrors of modern warfare.
- **E**vidence – the above quotation
- **C**omment – the poet uses frightening, repulsive images, invoking the senses of sight, taste and hearing, using harsh words with many *j*, *g*, *c*, *v* and *s* sounds. The 'gargling' metaphor stresses the unpleasantness of the situation. The images of cancer and sores contrast vividly with the reference to 'innocent tongues'.
- **S**cheme of things – the poet's purpose was to write realistically about the war. This was at a time when many of his contemporaries were writing patriotic verse which did not show the public what soldiers had to endure in the trenches.
- **I**nterpretation – although these are not pleasant lines to read, Owen achieves his purpose and underlines his point that poetry should tell the truth. As he wrote elsewhere, 'My subject is war and the pity of war. The poetry is in the pity.' The poetry achieves its effects through carefully chosen words, images and devices.

I said 'the SECSI way', not SEXY!

Language and devices in fiction (1–2)

Explain the techniques used by the author, Dylan Thomas, in the following extract from *The Outing: A Story*. What are the effects these techniques create? You should mention the use of images, onomatopoeia and alliteration and any other techniques you can identify. Quote details to support what you say. (20)

But there he was, always a steaming hulk of an uncle, his braces straining like hawsers, crammed behind the counter of the tiny shop at the front of the house, and breathing like a brass band; or guzzling and blustery in the kitchen over his gutsy supper, too big for everything except the great black boats of his boots. As he ate, the house grew smaller; he billowed out over the furniture, the loud check meadow of his waistcoat littered, as though after a picnic, with cigarette ends, peelings, cabbage stalks, bird's bones, gravy; and the forest fire of his hair crackled among the cooked hams from the ceiling.

The author uses an extended image (1), which compares his uncle to boats (1). He uses metaphors (1) – such as 'steaming hulk' (1), 'black boats of boots' (1) and 'billowed' (1) – and a simile (1), 'braces straining like hawsers' (1).

Alliteration is used (1) with many s sounds (1) which reinforce the boat images (1) as they create a sound which is like the wind or the sea (1). The same technique is used in the last part of the extract when the repeated letters f and c reinforce the references to fire and cooking through the onomatopoeic (1) blowing and crackling sounds they make (1).

Among this are scattered other lively images such as 'breathing like a brass band' (1) which also uses alliteration (1) to suggest the noisy wheezing the man made (1).

The other technique is to pile up long lists of words (1), such as in the reference to the picnic (1), which emphasises the larger-than-life nature of the man (1).

Dylan Thomas liked to use a large repertoire of vocabulary and unexpected imagery, often creating original and vivid pictorial effects – as in this passage. There is a great deal to comment on here. You should award yourself marks if you have identified features other than those noted above, provided you have commented on **effects** as well as usage.

TOTAL

STRUCTURE IN FICTION TEXTS (1)

Prose texts

The structure of a prose text will influence how you read, understand and react to it. Look at the beginning of this novel, *Push Me, Pull Me* by Sandra Chick:

> Everyone likes Christmas Eve. I don't. Would never admit it, though. Wouldn't be fair on the others to play selfish and dampen the spark. Truth is, I get jealous of the fun everybody else is having.

The writing is in the first person ('I'), in the voice or style of an invented teenage character. The effect is immediate and compelling. It feels as if you are being spoken to directly by someone who could be a friend of yours. The use of informal language (e.g. 'Would never admit it', 'Truth is') is a choice made by the author in structuring the story to appeal to its target audience.

Third-person narration ('he'/'she') can work equally well, especially if the structure allows for lots of dialogue. The advantage is that an author can exploit the contrast between formal description and speech so that readers do not tire of one style. Here is an example from *A Kestrel for a Knave* by Barry Hines:

> ...Jud was having his breakfast when Billy came downstairs. He glanced up at the clock. It was twenty-five to six.
>
> 'What's up wi' thee, shit t'bed?'
>
> 'I'm off out, nesting; wi' Tibby and Mac.'
>
> He whooshed the curtains open and switched the light off. The morning light came in clean as water, making them both look towards the window. The sun had not yet risen, but already the air was warm, and above the roof line of the house opposite, the chimney stack was silhouetted against a cloudless sky.
>
> 'It's a smashing morning again.'
>
> 'Tha wouldn't be saying that if tha wa' goin' where I'm goin'.'

A different structural approach to narrative is to use two or more characters as narrators. This approach can either use the straightforward alternation of chapters or sections, or use devices such as diaries or letters interspersed in the text. The main purpose of this is to give the reader more than one account of – or reaction to – events and characters. This encourages thoughtful and different interpretations of what apparently happens.

Other common structural devices such as flashbacks make you think about the sequence of events in a story, or the effect of the past on characters in the present. They may lead you to think 'What might have happened if…?'

Poetry texts

Look back at pages 13–14 to remind yourself of how the main structural features of a poem – rhyme, rhythm, layout of verses and choice of language – affect the reader's response to its meaning.

Drama texts

Look back at pages 17–18 to remind yourself of how dramatists may use a range of devices to structure scripts. Many of these are similar to prose structures – narrative viewpoint, contrasts in voice or language, chronological sequence, for example. However, there are a number of special effects available to radio, television and film in particular.

If you are comparing versions of a text in different media – for example, a film of a Shakespeare play or a stage dramatisation of a novel – consider whether the original structure has been changed at all. Have parts been left out, or additions made? Has the sequence of events been changed? Have the relationships of some of the characters changed? Why do you think this was done, and what effect does it have on you? A helpful way to think about the importance of how a text is structured is to consider what effect changes have had on it, or might have if they were made.

Structure in fiction texts (1–2)

1 Read this extract. How does the use of first-person narrative affect your reaction to the text? Think about the narrator's attitude to the reader (6) and the language, referring to examples to support your views (4).

> I suppose you'll want to know about everything. Where I was born, who my real parents are, when I was passed from lousy pillar to stinking post, why I'm small, how I became known as 'Oliver Twist' – but I don't feel like going into it. In the first place, that is all in the past, forgotten, buried. In the second place, how would you feel if you were my parents reading about what has happened to me?

2 How does the structure of this verse from William Blake's *A Poison Tree* help to convey the poem's meaning to the reader? (4)

> I was angry with my friend:
> I told my wrath, my wrath did end.
> I was angry with my foe:
> I told it not, my wrath did grow.

3 In the following direction from the television screenplay *Shop Thy Neighbour* by Alan Bleasdale, how does the writer use the medium to convey meaning to the viewer? (6)

> *[He crashes out of the room and down the stairs. We hear him banging into the back kitchen. We stay with Angie as she slumps on to the bed. We hear the kitchen door leading to the yard as it opens. We hear Chrissie crashing about. We see the children wake up. We see Angie looking up, then sitting up on the bed.]*

1 The opening gains your attention (1) by plunging straight into things (1) but is not willing to 'play the game' (1) by revealing personal details about the writer's childhood (1). The reference to Charles Dickens' Oliver Twist (1) shows that the narrator assumes the reader is intelligent/well read/has certain expectations of a first-person narrative (1).

The narrator addresses the reader directly as 'you' (1), making it sound like an intimate conversation (1). The use of slang words such as 'lousy' and 'stinking' (1) emphasises this directness/informality (1).

2 The use of rhymimg couplets (1) links the meaning of each pair of lines (1). The repetitive structure (1) helps to emphasise the minor but significant changes in each pair of lines (1).
Even very simple repetitive structures can have a function. Look out for texts where the seriousness of the meaning may appear to be at cross-purposes with the simplicity of the structure. This is a common device used by writers to gain the full attention of the reader. (For example, look again at the comment on the Margaret Atwood extract on page 30.)

3 Although no words are spoken, the sounds and camera direct our attention towards significant events (2). For example, we know that Chrissie is in a bad mood from the way he bangs around (1). We also know that Angie is upset when she slumps on the bed (1), then concerned about her children (1) when she sits up again as they awaken (1).
When commenting on structures in drama texts remember the obvious – they were written to be seen, rather than to be read. You therefore need to 'see' a performance in your mind's eye to judge the effect they have.

TOTAL

TYPES OF NON-FICTION TEXTS (1)

The main purpose of non-fiction texts is to convey **information or facts**, but this is often presented alongside the author's **ideas or opinions**. Look out for opinions disguised as facts (see page 49) and question the usefulness of arguments (see page 53).

Non-fiction texts include **autobiography**, **biography**, **journals**, **diaries**, **letters**, **essays** and **travel writing**. Because these deal with people's experiences, ideas and attitudes you should read them as though they were literary texts. The **language** used, the people, incidents, places or ideas described, are selected and structured in a **formal** way to have a particular effect on you. Many are written in the first person ('I') so your opinion of the author will influence judgements about the trustworthiness of the text.

In **biography**, the author often writes as though s/he knows all the innermost thoughts and qualities of the subject. You must decide how reliable the author is. In this excerpt, the author has a view of his subject as a businessman which was clearly not shared by everyone:

> Clark was unfairly blamed for the company's troubles, which derived from complacency, failure to modernise and restrictive practices.

You don't know which view is correct, but you must recognise that what is written here is merely an opinion. The opinion is backed by emotive and value-laden words such as 'unfairly', 'blamed', 'complacency', 'failure' and 'restrictive'.

Travel writing often reveals attitudes and prejudices. Paul Theroux in *The Kingdom by the Sea* shows his contempt for seaside holidaymakers, and perhaps some snobbery, when he describes Blackpool as:

> real clutter: the buildings that were not only ugly but also foolish and flimsy, the vacationers sitting under a dark sky with their shirts off, sleeping with their mouths open, emitting hog whimpers.

TYPES OF NON-FICTION TEXTS (2)

Words like 'clutter', 'ugly', 'foolish', 'flimsy' and 'hog whimpers' are intended to make you share Theroux's condescending view of these people who visit an unattractive place, sunbathe under 'a dark sky', look foolish and make animal noises. His use of the word 'emitting' puts you on Theroux's side: he knows you are an intelligent person who will understand his language and share his point of view – writers will try to manipulate you in this way.

Journals, **diaries** and **letters** are usually different. Sometimes they are written for publication (in which case you must read them in the way suggested above). More often they are informal in style and structure, and it is easier to spot the writer's opinions or prejudices. For example, Mary Shelley's diary entry for 6 March 1815 reads:

> Find my baby dead. Send for Hogg. Talk. A miserable day.
> In the evening read 'Fall of the Jesuits'. Hogg sleeps here.

The plain language, short sentences and jumps from one thought to another underline the spontaneity and real emotion in the writing.

Other non-fiction texts

These include information leaflets and other factual or informative writing, such as encyclopaedia articles or reference books. There is not always an author's name on these, but remember they have been written by someone. Look for evidence of bias in the language or in the selection and presentation of material.

Responding to non-fiction

You should comment on the language, content and structure of texts, and the influence of the author's own attitudes and ideas. Remember to answer these questions:
● What do I feel about the text?
● Does it successfully achieve its purpose?

Types of non-fiction texts (1–2)

1 Explain three ways in which the style of an autobiography might differ from that of a diary (3).

2 Read this extract from a travel book.
   (a) Explain the author's attitude towards the place and list the words which convey it (8).
   (b) Why has the author chosen to describe these features of the place? (4)

> It was a summer afternoon but so stormy and dark the street lamps were on, and so were the lights in the train. Even the sea was grim here – not rough but motionless and oily, a sort of offshore soup made of sewage and poison.

3 Read the following extract from the review of a new car.
   (a) List three pieces of information it gives you (3).
   (b) Explain how the piece also reveals two of the writer's own attitudes (2).

> Engine noise is intrusive both at rest and at speed. The 0–60 mph sprint takes a soporific 15.8 sec so, as often as not, you drive with the accelerator pressed to the floor. And that, we suspect, is the reason most owners won't come close to Citroen's claimed combined fuel figure of 44.1 mpg.

1 The language of an autobiography is likely to be more formal than that of a diary (1); an autobiography will be more structured (or the material will be more carefully selected) than in a diary (1); the writer's opinions are likely to be more open or obvious in a diary (1).

2 (a) The writer sees the place as thoroughly unattractive (1). This is conveyed particularly by the words 'stormy' (1), 'dark' (1), 'grim' (1), 'motionless' (1), 'oily' (1), 'sewage' (1) and 'poison' (1).

(b) He mentions the contrast between the season and the weather (1) to emphasise how miserable the place is (1) and the appearance of the sea (1) because it is particularly unappealing (1).

Look for unusual or unexpected words and images when set a question like this. The writer is describing a seaside resort in summer, so the words listed in answer **(a)** are not what you would expect. In answering part **(b)**, you should realise that the aspects of the place the writer chooses to describe are those that you might expect (the weather and the sea), so this reinforces the awfulness of the place.

3 (a) Three pieces of information are that engine noise is intrusive (1), that the car goes from 0–60 in 15.8 seconds (1) and that the combined fuel figure is 44.1 mpg (1).

(b) The writer's own attitudes are that he does not like engine noise as he calls it 'intrusive' (1) and that he prefers faster cars, as he calls the acceleration of this one 'soporific' (sleepy) (1).

These questions test your ability to identify fact and opinion, which is never as easy as it sounds. For example, is describing the engine noise as 'intrusive' a piece of (factual) information, or merely the writer's opinion? On balance, it probably qualifies as information, since the engine is clearly noisy, although some might find it less annoying than the writer did, which is why his dislike of engine noise generally can be labelled as an opinion (or attitude).

TOTAL

Media texts include radio, film, television, magazines and newspapers. They may contain both fiction (e.g. realisations of a classic novel as drama script or printed cartoon) and non-fiction materials (e.g. advertisements).

In your GCSE English exam, you are most likely to encounter non-fiction, print-based materials. In responding to them, you need to explain how particular effects are achieved. You should also comment on why texts are successful in relation to their target **audience** and intended **purpose**.

Audience

Many media texts are aimed at broad groups of people, categorised by income, profession or interests. Particular advertisements, for example, will be aimed at different groups and will therefore be presented and distributed differently. Rolls Royce cars are not advertised on prime-time commercial television, but Skodas are. This allows the authors of media texts to make certain assumptions about the audience's beliefs, lifestyles and aspirations. For example, an article in a magazine for members of the National Farmers' Union begins:

> British food is clearly the best, and how to prove it beyond doubt to supermarkets, caterers and the general public, is the aim of a new industry-wide farm standards initiative being promoted by NFU.

This is neither a lively nor balanced presentation of views. The writer is addressing an audience assumed to be both interested and sympathetic.

Purpose

In the most successful media texts, purpose is hardly distinguishable from audience, as media authors need to give their audiences what they want. This is why media texts may often seem stereotypical: for example, magazines aimed at men are full of articles about sport and cars, and magazines aimed at women are about fashion, food and children.

A tabloid newspaper shows a picture of Gianfranco Zola, Chelsea's Italian footballer, serving a pizza under the headline:

which contains the puns typical of the medium, but also presents a stereotypical view of Italians. Even more 'upmarket' broadsheet newspapers use similar approaches, as in this headline from *The Independent*: 'FRENCH SAY NON TO LE BUSINESS SPEAK ANGLAIS'. This is designed to capture the interest of an educated readership. It also sustains the supposed hostility between the French and the English.

Media language

Media texts are often short and snappy. They are designed to grab the reader's attention. You should therefore look out for, and comment on, language which

- tries to influence your opinion (e.g. 'clearly' in the NFU article)
- sounds memorable, but has no real meaning (e.g. 'Mr Muscle loves the jobs you hate')
- is partly truthful (e.g. 'kills all *known* germs')
- appeals to snobbery or fear (e.g. words such as 'exclusive'), or mentions of 'understains' in washing powder advertisements.

Structural and presentational devices

Comment on how titles, subheadings, frames, colour, font styles and sizes, and illustrations are used to catch and direct the reader's interest. Charts and diagrams may be as important as words in conveying information.

Media texts (1–2)

1 (a) Describe the intended audience and purpose for this advertisement, referring to the content, language and any other features to support your argument (11).

(b) Suggest the type of publication in which this advertisement might have appeared, and give reasons for your suggestion (3).

And for those who have everything

Designed to enable you to work from home, The Xerox Document HomeCentre combines the work of a colour inkjet printer, an instant colour photocopier and a colour scanner.

You can slide any document through the front and it will transfer the image to your PC and translate it into text through the software provided. The scanner is also detachable which means you can scan books too.

The WorkCentre, which is the same price, also combines the use of a fax.

Price: £499 (plus VAT)

2 (a) What is the purpose of this cartoon and what audience do you think it is aimed at? (3)

(b) Suggest the type of publication in which it might have appeared, and give reasons for your suggestion (3).

'What's happened to Deirdre in Coronation Street?'

1 (a) The audience for this advertisement will be educated (1) and fairly well-off (1) business people (1) who work from home (1), are computer-literate (1) and write reports or other documents (1). The illustration suggests a modern home office (1), with the computer, large desk and flowers (1) all reinforcing the image of a comfortable lifestyle (1). The headline appeals to snobbery (1), although in a gently humorous way (1).

(b) This advertisement probably appeared in a newspaper or magazine read by well-off business people (1) as it assumes they will be interested in the product (1) and would be able to afford the price (1).

In fact, it was in the *Independent on Sunday* as part of a series which advertises the latest technological gadgets to readers. It is clearly not from a computer magazine, as the language used is not technical, and there is no detailed explanation of how it works or of how effectively it does all the different jobs – in fact, you might have commented that it is being sold more like a fashion accessory than a piece of IT equipment.

2 (a) It is principally to amuse the reader (1), but also to make the reader feel part of a group with similar interests (1); it is therefore aimed at those who watch soap operas on television, particularly *Coronation Street* (1).

(b) It probably comes from a newspaper, or maybe a television listings magazine, with a large readership (1) including many people who watch soap operas (1). It is most likely to come from a tabloid newspaper (1).

That is a perfectly reasonable answer: surprisingly, however, the cartoon was from *The Telegraph*, a broadsheet paper with a largely middle-class readership. It just goes to show how much *Coronation Street* has wheedled its way into the consciousness of the whole nation.

TOTAL

Definite facts do not often appear in written texts, even those labelled 'non-fiction'. Look at this simple advertisement for a credit card:

The only facts in it are the (approximate) number of outlets and the telephone number. All the rest is opinion (even 'your *local* branch' might be a long way to people who live in the country). This advertisement is designed to make the reader feel that it is important to own one of these cards.

Creating atmosphere

In the following excerpt from Reginald Thompson's newspaper account of skirmishes in North Korea, there is very little fact at all. The writer's purpose is to establish the atmosphere or 'feel' of the event, before going on to relay the bare facts of what actually happened.

Cry Korea

It was a game of blind man's bluff in these wild rugged irregular hills in which the enemy moved freely, easily eluding the groping arms of the Americans by day, and swooping down upon them, blind in the night, with devastating fury and magnificent discipline.

You may not be asked to identify fact and opinion directly. Instead you might be asked to describe what a text tells you about something, and then to explain what the author feels about it. In other words, first tell the facts, then consider the opinions. Remember to use your common sense. For example, if a house advertisement claims that the residence has 'a large south-facing garden', it is reasonable to assume that the property has a garden and that it will (more or less) face south. Whether it is large or not is more likely to be a matter of opinion.

SAUNTON

NEW INSTRUCTION

£249,000
- Magnificently situated individual detached house
- Large south-facing garden • Central heating
- 4 bedrooms • 2 receptions • Bathroom
- Shower room • Cloaks • Detached garage
- Approx 1 acre

Travel writing

In examinations, you may be presented with a piece of travel writing. This is a genre (type of writing) in which facts, opinions and the writer's ideas and attitudes are often intermingled. Sorting out one from the other requires careful reading. Read this extract from *Please Don't Call it Soviet Georgia* by Mary Russell carefully:

> The silence is heavy with waiting. Then it comes, faint at first. A heavy, rumbling sound. A film of nervous sweat breaks out across my back. Maybe it's not tanks. Maybe it's aircraft going over. At this time of night? No, the tanks rumble on, thunder into our ears. Below, the faces are impassive, unflinching. Beside me, a young woman puts her arms round her friend who is sobbing. Suddenly, the sound stops. It's true, there was nothing to fear. Not this time. It was a tape, the tape of what happened last year. Only, last year the tanks didn't stop...

The facts are few – she is scared by what she thinks are tanks. But the emotions, attitudes and values (the opinions) are what make the writing moving and powerful.

Fact and opinion (1–2)

1 Read the following report about the Vietnam War by Gavin
Young, entitled *Slow Boats to China*. Identify six facts (6) and
four opinions (4).

> In 1965, before the American forces landed en masse in
> Vietnam, the Vietnamese Army seemed to be heading for
> total destruction; it was losing a battalion or two every
> week, most of them in engagements very close to Saigon.
> One day I travelled from Saigon to the riverside township of
> My To, south of the capital, in a bus crowded with
> Vietnamese civilians and soldiers; bundles of shopping and
> chickens cluttered the floor under the seats.

2 Read the following piece of travel writing, from *The Hidden Land*
by Ursula Graham Bower. Find five facts (5), three opinions (3)
and two statements which might be either (2).

> Calcutta was hotter than the hobs of hell and plague,
> cholera and smallpox were all raging. The travel agents
> were at a standstill because of strikes. Tim went from end to
> end of the city in a rickshaw, getting permits for every
> conceivable item of baggage. Independence here meant
> bureaucracy run mad . . .. You could take out six polo-sticks
> and several tennis-rackets, but only one pair of spectacles,
> and we had to get a separate permit for my gold wedding-
> ring. When we came to leave, nobody looked at any of them.
> We took off from Dum-Dum in the early morning, the
> chequered table of the earth wheeling and shrinking and
> falling behind, and half our lives was over, cast off and torn
> away and shredded into the dust of India below.

1 The **facts** are:

- The Vietnam War was in progress in 1965/a large number of American troops landed in Vietnam in 1965.
- Battles were taking place near to Saigon.
- My To is a riverside place/is south of Saigon.
- Saigon is the capital.
- You can travel to My To from Saigon by bus.
- There were civilians and soldiers on the bus with Gavin Young.

Opinions:

- The Vietnamese Army seemed to be heading for total destruction.
- It was losing a battalion or two every week.
- The bus was crowded.
- The floor of the bus was cluttered.

Note how some of the facts have to be assumed (e.g. that the war was happening in 1965 and that there was a bus from Saigon to My To). We are not told directly either of these things, but they must be true.

2 Facts:

- There was disease in Calcutta.
- There were strikes at travel agents.
- Tim collected luggage permits.
- Nobody looked at the permits when they left.
- The plane took off in the early morning/from Dum-Dum.

Opinions:

- Calcutta was hotter than the hobs of hell.
- Plague and cholera were raging.
- Independence here meant bureacracy run made . . .

Statements which could be **fact or opinion** are:

- Details of what you were allowed to take out of India
- Half our lives was over…

When reading non-fiction texts, you often need to follow an argument or train of thought. This will help you to understand the writer's purpose, or understand what the writer is trying to persuade or instruct you about. Such pieces of text might be:

● an article about bloodsports
● a set of instructions for constructing an item of furniture
● an advertisement.

Look out for the effect of structural features which organise the writing. For example, the use of headlines, subheadings, numbers, diagrams and pictures, or flowcharts (see pages 57–58 and 61–62 for more detail about these). These features shape your response to the writing. Look at this card designed and produced by British Telecom to be carried by mobile phone users to remind them of certain facilities on their phone.

Useful Numbers

Carry this card with you for some useful numbers to call from your mobile.

Free Numbers

Cellnet Customer Care	- 100 **SEND**
Emergency Services	- 112 or 999 **SEND**

Standard Charged Numbers

Talking Pages	- 888 **SEND**
National Rail Enquiries	- 0345 48 49 50 **SEND**
AA Breakdown	- 2505 SEND
RAC Breakdown	- 4505 SEND

Premium Rate Numbers

Directory Enquiries	- 192 SEND
AA Roadwatch	- 401 100 SEND
UK Met Office Weathercall	- 0891 232 770 SEND

Note: If your tariff package does not allow Premium Rate calls but you need the service please call your BT Mobile customer service team. The Directory Enquiries service (192) is available to all customers.

Callback

Callback has no connection or subscription charges. Access to your Callback mailbox or message retrieval is charged at 39p per minute (inc. VAT).

To switch Callback On	- 1750 SEND
To switch Callback Off	- 1760 SEND
To listen to your messages	- 901 SEND

You can leave a direct message in the mailbox of other Cellnet customers by dialling their mobile number (excluding the initial zero) then SEND when their service is On or Off.

To access advanced features:

Press 901 SEND
During the greeting or message press ✳
Wait for prompt
Enter your PIN number (initially set to 8705)
You are now in 'Command Mode' and can press:

1 - to hear the menu options
2 - to retrieve and delete messages
3 - to lock your mailbox
6 - to change your mailbox PIN
7 - to change your personal greeting
8 - to change new message notification

BT 1934 12/97

The clarity of the BT card is aided by:

- brief instructions
- plain language
- clear sequencing
- the bold headline which separates the 'advanced features' section.

Note how not all the instructions on the card are grammatically complete (e.g. 'Wait for prompt'). This helps to keep the instructions short and precise.

Technical language

Of course, not all arguments or instructions can be put into simple or brief language. Complex ideas need a full explanation. They may require the use of **technical language**. Look at this extract from a buyer's guide to four-wheel drive vehicles (*The Essential Guide to Choosing and Using Your 4×4 Vehicle*, published by the Rover Group Ltd):

All cars and 4x4s use at least one differential. This set of gears transfers power from the transmission to the wheels (often through a 90-degree angle), whilst allowing wheels on the same axle to turn at different speeds. The latter fact is vital since when a vehicle takes a corner, all four wheels travel at different speeds and follow different lines.

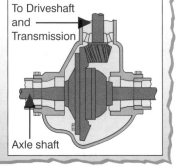

To Driveshaft and Transmission

Axle shaft

A typical rear differential

Although the language is reasonably straightforward, the ideas are not necessarily easy for someone who does not understand the workings of power units in cars. The diagram does not seem to make the argument any easier, as the labels include some terms not used in the writing. Be prepared to identify failures as well as successes – provided you can explain why.

Following an argument (1–2)

1 Compare the helpfulness and practicality of the two recipes below. Look at features such as information (5), language (6), and presentation (3).

A

Luxury Hot Chocolate

Lovely and comforting on a nasty cold evening or after a long country walk in the winter.

Preparation and cooking time: 5 minutes

❖ 2–3 squares chocolate (optional)
❖ 1/2 pt/300ml milk
❖ 1 tbsp drinking chocolate
❖ 3 or 4 marshmallows (optional)

Toppings:

❖ 1 tbsp pouring cream, whipped cream or aerosol cream
❖ Shake of drinking chocolate or grated chocolate (or both!)
❖ Chocolate flake (optional)
❖ 1 or 2 marshmallows (optional)

Break chocolate squares, if used, into a mug. Heat milk to almost boiling point and pour into mug, add drinking chocolate and marshmallows, if used, and stir until dissolved. Top with cream and decorate with drinking or grated chocolate, chocolate flake and halved marshmallows, if liked. Serve at once, while lovely and hot.

B

TOASTED PUMPKIN SEED AND CHILLI DIP

PREPARATION TIME: 8 minutes plus 1 hour standing
COOKING: 4 minutes

SERVES 4
NOT SUITABLE FOR FREEZING

50g pumpkin seeds	1 red chilli, finely chopped
200ml Greek-style yoghurt	1/2 tblsp paprika
3 tblsp mild chilli powder	seasoning
2 tblsp chopped fresh coriander	

1 Place the pumpkin seeds in a small pan, cover with a tight-fitting lid and cook for 3–4 minutes until they are well toasted, shaking the pan occasionally to prevent the seeds from burning.
2 Put the pumpkin seeds into a food processor or blender and process to a fine powder. Add the yoghurt, paprika and chilli powder and process for a few seconds until all the ingredients are incorporated.
3 Stir in the chopped chilli and coriander and season to taste. If possible, leave for about an hour before eating to allow the flavours to develop. Spoon the dip into a bowl and serve with tortilla chips and crudités.

PER SERVING: 139 calories
Fibre 1g, Carbohydrate 4g, Fat 11g, Saturated fat 4g, Protein 7g, Added sugar none, Salt 0.19g.

2 What does the writer of the following suggest about the actor's character? (6)

> **Raymond Huntley** was a shy, private man, not easy to know, but behind a mask of intolerance – his old friends maintained – was a dry sense of humour and great kindness.

from *The Daily Telegraph*, 18 June 1990

1 The information in recipe A is imprecise (1). For example, in the quantities of ingredients required/whether certain ingredients are used at all (1). Recipe B is quite precise (1). It even gives nutritional information (1) and a portion cost (1).

The language of recipe A is simple/straightforward (1) but is sometimes descriptive rather than practical (1). For example, the use of the word 'lovely' (1). Recipe B is business-like/practical (1), although there are some less precise words (1), such as 'occasionally' (1).

Ingredients are clearly listed in both recipes (1), but the numbered steps (1) in recipe B make it more attractive and easier to follow (1).
Look also at pages 57–68. The structure, presentational devices and language used in non-fiction texts are crucial to their success in putting over an argument or point of view.

2 The writer suggests that the actor seemed to be unfriendly (1) and/or short-tempered (1) but this was only an act (1). The actor was in fact sympathetic (1) and amusing (1) according to friends who had known him for a long time (1).
The writer leaves you wondering what the actor, Raymond Huntley, was really like. If he had old friends who liked him, can he have been so intolerant? The fact that the writer includes the reference to 'his old friends' suggests that, in his/her view, most people who met the actor would not have shared their opinion.

TOTAL

Most non-fiction and media texts are put together carefully so as to have maximum impact on their intended audiences. This is true even of 'private' texts such as diaries or letters, which will usually be structured in narrative or chronological ways to capture the writer's idea or point of view. More 'public' texts – such as information leaflets or magazine articles – will usually show a wide range of features. This is because there are often business-related reasons for their need to succeed.

Most of these additional features are intended to ensure that the reader understands the message or purpose of the text in two main ways. Firstly, by presenting information in a logical way and/or in a way which will capture your interest and imagination. Secondly, by presenting text in small units so that you are able to take it in easily and think about it as you go. You are less likely to become bored by it, and more likely to stick with it to the end. Breaking text up in this way also allows it to be presented attractively (as you will see in more detail on pages 61–62).

Look at this advertisement for homes in the USA:

Florida

Largest selection of 3, 4 and 5 bedroom houses in Orlando, New Port Richey, South West Gulf Coast

★ 3 bedroom pool homes from $125,000
★ 4 bedroom pool homes from $145,000
★ Golf course developments
★ 80% mortgages available
★ Full management and rental services

For information pack:
Tel: 01432 992655   Fax: 01432 793353

F.J. Cook & Sons

This example shows use of the following structural features:

● A clear heading to attract the attention of targeted readers.

● Although there is only a small amount of text, it is full of relevant information.

● Key details are in a bullet-pointed list to avoid information overload.

● Different aspects of the information (e.g. contacts for further details) are separated to help readers easily find what they need to know.

These are some of the most common structural devices found in printed non-fiction/media texts – whatever their length, purpose or audience.

Other devices

Other devices to look out for include the use of graphical information (particularly charts or tables) to convey numerical or financial information, or maps, diagrams and timetables to convey travel information.

The purpose of such structural devices is to ensure that the reader quickly gains whatever information the writer wishes to convey. When responding to non-fiction/media texts you should always write about structural features with these questions in mind:

● Does the structuring of the content help the writer achieve the desired purpose?

● If so, how? If not, what are the shortcomings of the structure?

● What effect is this text likely to have on its target audience?

The last point is important. If a piece of text is aimed, say, at teenagers then it is not reasonable to criticise it on the grounds that older people would not understand the use of slang or colloquial language. Similarly, do not criticise an advertisement for pensions aimed at older people because it is 'boring' to a teenage reader.

Structure in non-fiction texts (1–2)

1 (a) Identify five structural features used in this advertisement for a house to let (5).

(b) Comment on how they might help it achieve the desired effect on its target audience (5).

Howard Prince Stepney & Partners

THE INTERNATIONAL LETTING AGENCY

Windsor • Cheam • Richmond

TO LET

Superb contemporary four bedroom house on the banks of the River Thames within walking distance of Richmond

£5,500 pcm

Telephone: 0181 498 3144

---

2 (a) Identify five structural features in this information from *What Car?* magazine (5).

(b) Comment on their effectiveness (5).

Car supermarket shopping – and main dealer prices						
Car supermarket	**Make/model**	**Year**	**Market price**	**Dealer price**	**Saved**	
Sanderson Motorhouse, Cheltenham	Ford Mondeo 1.8 LX 5dr	97R	£10,995	£11,495	£500	
	Vauxhall Vectra 1.8 LS 5dr	97R	£10,995	£11,295	£300	
Car Supermarket, Newport **Best Deal**	Ford Mondeo 1.8 LX 5dr	97R	£10,799	£11,495	£696	
	Vauxhall Vectra 1.8 LS 5dr	97R	£10,595	£11,295	£700	
Lex Autosales, Bristol	Ford Mondeo 1.8 LX TD	96P	£8999	£9945	£946	
	Peugeot 406 1.9 L TD	96P	£9489	£10,195	£706	
Discount Cars Direct, Sunningdale	Ford Mondeo 2.0 GLX 5dr	97P	£10,299	£11,495	£1196	
	Vauxhall Vectra 1.8 LS 5dr	97P	£9999	£10,795	£796	
Carland, Thurrock	Ford Mondeo 1.8 LX 5dr	97P	£10,800	£11,095	£295	
	Vauxhall Vectra 1.8 GLS 5dr	97P	£10,500	£10,995	£495	

1 **(a)** Structural features:
- main heading (1)
- bullet pointing (1)
- brief text (1)
- use of abbreviation (1)
- telephone number separate (1).

(b) The main heading makes the purpose/audience of the advertisement clear (1). Bullet-pointing the locations of the firm makes it easy for readers to see if there is a branch convenient for them (1). The text about the house is brief but it contains sufficient information for readers to decide if it interests them (1). An abbreviation ('pcm': per calendar month) is used which saves space and would be understood by the target audience (1). The telephone number of the firm is separate and in **bold** to encourage readers to follow up the advertisement (1). Notice how all the comments are related to the **audience** and **purpose** of the advertisement. When you are reading any non-fiction/media text, make sure that one of the first decisions you make is to identify the purpose and target audience. This will make it easier for you to comment on the effectiveness of the techniques used.

2 **(a)** Structural features:
- clear main heading (1)
- use of table (1)
- column headings (1)
- brief text (1)
- use of a flash (1).

(b) The clear main heading sets out the purpose of the information (1).
The use of a table enables an easy comparison of the information in the text (1).
Column headings further clarify the information (1).
The text itself is very brief and so guides the reader to the most significant information (1).
The use of the 'Best Deal' flash quickly draws the reader's attention to the highlight of the information (1).

TOTAL

These are more to do with how the text is presented. There is some overlap here with structural devices (see pages 57–58). For example, bullet points or headlines are really both structural and presentational. All the devices discussed on page 58, and those detailed here, are concerned with achieving desired effects on particular audiences. You should therefore respond to the use of presentational devices in the same way as to structural devices. You should ask yourself these questions:

● Do the devices help the writer to achieve the desired purpose?
● If so, how? If not, why have the devices not worked?
● What effect is this text likely to have on its target audience?

Frames

These may be placed around parts of a text, or around the whole text. The effect in either case should be to draw the reader's eye to something significant. Look out for which parts of a text are highlighted in this way and which are not. Sometimes the absence of frames can be used to divert attention from details which the writer does not want to stand out – such as details of additional charges or product guarantees.

Illustrations

These may serve a number of purposes. Above all, they can make dull text look more attractive and therefore more interesting. At the same time, they may present an image of the information, product or idea which the writer is trying to promote. Consider how realistic or honest illustrations are – sometimes new cars or houses will be represented by an 'artist's impression'. Ask yourself 'why?' Is it because the actual product doesn't exist? Or can the 'impression' impress more than the real thing?

Colour

Colour is often used sparingly (as in this book) as it is expensive to reproduce. Although colour can make text eye-catching (see poster on page 61), over-fussy or poor use of colours can be distracting. They can make text more difficult to read, rather than more attractive.

Fonts

The style and size of **different fonts** may affect the way a reader reacts to text. For example, some fonts have a more 'serious' or formal appearance, while others are more obviously informal. Some styles are associated closely with particular eras (e.g. the 1970s or 1980s) or even individual products. Some styles may be associated with feelings or atmospheres. For example, a ruined castle, or a horror film, might use a 'gothic' or 'medieval' font in their promotional literature. Larger fonts may be used to emphasise particular aspects of a text. The so-called 'small print' may hide less attractive information. Text may be in **bold**, in *italics* or <u>underlined</u> in various ways, to add to the impact of different font styles and sizes.

𝕲𝔥𝔬𝔰𝔱 𝔗𝔯𝔞𝔦𝔫

Logos and symbols

Logos are used mostly to fix the image of a company or organisation in the reader's mind so that it is instantly recognised when met again.

Some advertising relies on well-known logos and does not mention the company name at all. The effect of this can be to make the  reader feel as though s/he belongs almost to an exclusive 'club' of those who understand the logo, and can therefore make them more responsive to the advertisement. Symbols such as ticks, crosses, pairs of scissors and so on can be space-savers, and thus cost-savers. They can also be helpful to readers.

Presentational devices (1–2)

1 (a) In this advertisement for home insurance, identify five presentational and/or structural features (5).

(b) Comment on how each feature contributes to the success of the advertisement (5).

Discount type	% discount
Approved alarm fitted †	5%
Approved security locks fitted* †	5%
Any applicant aged 50 or over	5%
Joint buildings and contents policy	10%
An excess is the first part of any claim you have to pay. You may choose to change the standard £50 excess to one of the following:	
£25	£5 annual charge
£100	5% discount
£200	12.5% discount
Please note the excess for personal belongings and pedal cycles is £25 and this cannot be charged. * The discount does not apply in areas where we require certain extra security measures. † Ask for a copy of our Minimum Standard of Security leaflet to check if you qualify for our alarm and security locks discounts.	

2 (a) Identify five presentational features used in this advertisement (5).

(b) Comment on how effectively they attract the attention of an appropriate target audience (5).

 THE COPPER KETTLE COFFEE SHOP

WHITE ROCK FALLS

Visit the newly refurbished **Visitors Centre**
(with educational 'hands-on' exhibition)*
Relax over coffee or a light lunch in our new Coffee Shop
where emphasis is on value for money
and a warm welcome awaits visitors and locals a like.

Opening times:
End of Oct. – 1 April   Mon – Fri 10am – 4pm
1 April – end of Oct.   7 days a week 10am – 5pm
For more information or a sample menu ring: 01699 336426
*Child friendly and with access for the disabled

1 (a) Presentational/structural features:
- table format (1)
- reversed colours of the column headings (1)
- font used (1)
- words simple and straightforward (1)
- footnotes (1).

(b) A table format is used to clarify what could be complicated information (1).

The reversed colours of the column headings make them stand out as titles (1).

The font used is simple and 'clean' for ease of reading/so as not to distract the reader's attention from the potentially complicated text (1).

The words in the text are straightforward to keep the message as simple as possible (1).

Footnotes are used to clarify and extend the information where necessary or to keep unnecessary extra words out of the main table (1).

This is an example of text which is unlikely to be exciting, given its subject matter and the need to convey detailed information. However, the controlled use of appropriate structures and presentational devices can make the text effective and efficient.

2 (a) Presentational features:
- decorative frame (1)
- upper case headlines (1)
- teacup logo (1)
- some use of text in bold (1)
- short paragraphs (1).

(b) The decorative frame makes the advertisement stand out (1).

The upper case headlines make the location of the coffee shop clear (1).

The teacup logo shows the nature of the advertisement at a glance and attracts the target audience immediately (1).

Some use of **bold** type emphasises important details (1).

Short paragraphs break up the text for easy reading (1).

TOTAL

All texts are written for a purpose. Skilful writers will manipulate (i.e. control) your response to a text through the range of techniques they use. You have already looked at some of these techniques, but the most valuable weapon a writer has is individual words. Look at this fairly typical advertisement for a new house:

Large detached house with four double bedrooms, all with bathrooms.

Set in a charming village environment.

Convenient access to M4.

Home exchange available.

£349,950

Similar housetypes to be built

Honeypot Grove, Holywell, Berkshire

Follow signs towards Holywell from junction 8/9 off the M4.

Sales office and superb showhome open from 10am to 6pm, Thursday to Tuesday (Monday 2pm to 6pm)

Tel: 01826 7006213

Individual words such as 'large', 'detached', 'charming', 'convenient' and 'superb' are all examples of opinions disguised as facts. There are also whole phrases designed to influence the reader's feelings:

- 'charming village environment' is intended to evoke a warm glow of belonging to a community with old-fashioned values;
- 'convenient access to M4' shows that the house isn't too far away from the city;
- 'home exchange available' reassures the prospective buyer that they won't need to sell their existing house.

However, note the words in very small print beneath the illustration – 'Similar housetypes to be built'. This is not avoiding the truth, but it does point to the fact that the picture is not actually the house for sale.

LANGUAGE IN NON-FICTION TEXTS (2)

The language of non-fiction, particularly that of advertisements, often appeals to our emotions, such as snobbery. The house advertisement on page 65 does that. Although the language is restrained (i.e. not 'over the top'), it nevertheless suggests that this is a house for a successful businessperson.

Other types of non-fiction texts, such as autobiography or travel writing, often use language in a more literary way. This is intended to engage the reader's imagination. As an example, Roald Dahl mentions in *Going Solo*:

> sinister vultures waiting like feathered undertakers for death to come along and give them something to work on.

Humour is often used in texts like these. It may be kindly or, more often than not, pointed and condemning. Read this extract from *Notes From a Small Island* by Bill Bryson:

> Bradford's role in life is to make every place else in the world look better in comparison, and it does this very well.

When commenting on humour remember to explain the effect it has on the reader. Is it to make a sort of bond between the writer and reader? Or is it to make sharp criticism of someone or something? Or is it just to show off the author's verbal dexterity (clever use of words)?

Verbal dexterity is often used by writers of media texts which advertise products. '**Catchphrases**' which become associated with chocolate bars or soft drinks are important to the success of one kind of non-fiction writer. The idea is to fix certain products in our minds by coming up with memorable phrases. These 'catchphrases' rely on devices such as rhyme and repetition ('A Mars a day helps you work, rest and play') or literary language that is slightly ridiculous (such as describing an Australian lager as the 'amber nectar'). Alliteration, puns, onomatopoeia and (often far-fetched) imagery are all used by writers when advertising products. (Look back at pages 9–10 to remind yourself of these devices and the effects they can achieve.)

Language in non-fiction texts (1–2)

1 Look at this restaurant advertisement.
 (a) Pick out four examples of language designed to have a
     particular effect on the reader (4).
 (b) Comment on how this language does appeal to the
     reader (4).

SHAWS RESTAURANT HAWES

Fine continental cuisine served in charming surroundings.
The menu offers plenty of interesting and intriguing combinations
professionally prepared for you by our chef **Anton Deschamps**

Open Tuesday to Sunday – evening and lunches

Please book for weekend meals to avoid disappointment.

To book your table tel 01699 745866

---

2 In this extract from *And when did you last see your father?* the
 author, Blake Morrison, evokes various feelings through his use
 of language.
 (a) Identify and comment on three examples which make the
     underground train seem threatening (6).
 (b) Identify and comment on three examples which describe
     the people around him (6)

...then I hear the inevitable growling and swelling in the tunnel,
the sleek rat springing hyperactive and lethal from its trap. The
carriage is full of men, every one a killer, brow-lines of rage and
torment sculpted as if with hammer and chisel. Next to me is a
close-cropped twenty-year-old in a leather jacket, with an AIDS
INTERNATIONAL DAY sticker. He crouches by the pneumatic
doors next to his dog, a beautiful grey velvety Weimaraner. The
dog is nervous to be travelling in this thing, the rattling steel,
the shaky floor. Every so often it gives a little howl, and when it
does its leathered owner yanks on its collar and pulls its face up
hard against his, staring it out, boss, disciplinarian, torturer.

---

1 (a) Language:
- 'fine continental cuisine' (1)
- 'charming surroundings' (1)
- 'interesting and intriguing combinations' (1)
- 'professionally prepared' (1).

(b) Comments:
- 'Fine continental cuisine' appeals to readers who believe they have a taste for sophisticated food (1).
- 'Charming surroundings' appeals to readers' appreciation of an appealing environment (1).
- 'Interesting and intriguing combinations' appeals to readers who feel they are adventurous in their eating habits (1).
- 'Professionally prepared' appeals to readers who believe they are entitled to the best (1).

This advertisement is geared at appealing to a gentle kind of snobbery among its readers. Providing the name of the chef is another example of this, which you might have picked out. Also the suggestion that you might need to book at weekends to avoid disappointment.

2 (a) The train:
- 'growling and swelling' (1) gives the train the sound of a fierce creature (1)
- '...the sleek rat...trap' (1) continues the idea of an attacking creature (1)
- 'the rattling steel, the shaky floor' (1) makes the train seem insecure, unsafe, even dangerous (1).

(b) The people:
- 'every one a killer...hammer and chisel' (1) makes the men sound violent and aggressive (1)
- 'leathered owner' (1) makes the man sound tough and uncaring (1)
- 'boss, disciplinarian, torturer' (1) reinforces the previous images by making this man sound uncaring, cruel and selfish (1).

TOTAL

Spelling (1)

Learning spellings and spelling unknown words

If you are learning a new spelling first **LOOK** at it (to see if it reminds you of any other words or spelling patterns you already know), then **COVER** it (and try to 'see' the word in your mind's eye), then **WRITE** it (from memory) and finally **CHECK** it (to see if you were right).

If you have to spell a difficult or new word from memory or from just hearing it, **LISTEN** to its sound (say it slowly to yourself several times) and think which letters might represent those sounds; **THINK** about spelling rules or patterns you know; **WRITE** down two or three spellings which might be correct then decide which looks or 'feels' right. Finally **CHECK** in a dictionary/spellchecker.

You won't always be able to use a spellchecker or a dictionary or ask someone how to spell a word, especially in an exam. So learn to:
● think about word families: if you can spell *appear*, you shouldn't have problems with *disappear, disappearing, disappeared*, and so on;
● think about word origins: you shouldn't forget the *n* in 'government' if you remember that its job is to *govern* us.

Spelling rules

● *q* is always followed by *u*, except in *Iraq*

● *i* comes before *e* except when it follows *c* (e.g. *friend, brief*, but *ceiling, receive*)

● If *all* is followed by another syllable, it loses one *l* (e.g. *also, already, always*; but note that *all right* must be written as two words)

● If a word ends with a single vowel followed by a single consonant, you must double the consonant if adding an ending which begins with a vowel (e.g. *shop–shopped–shopping; swim–swimmer–swimming*)

● If you add *full* or *till* to the end of another word or syllable, you must drop one *l* (e.g. *hopeful, until*).

SPELLING (2)

More spelling rules

- Drop the final *e* from a word if adding an ending which starts with a vowel (e.g. *love–loving; rattle–rattling*)

- Keep the final *e* in a word if adding an ending which begins with a consonant (e.g. *love–lovely; rattle–rattled*)

- If a word ends with a consonant followed by *y*, change the *y* to *i* before all endings except *ing* (e.g. *funny–funnily; marry–married–marrying*)

- An *i* or *ee* sound at the end of a word is nearly always shown by the letter *y* (e.g. *country, hungry*, but common exceptions are *coffee, committee* and *taxi* as well as foreign borrowings, especially Italian words such as *macaroni* and *spaghetti*)

- The *i before e except after c* rule is generally true, but not if the sound is *ay* (e.g. *neighbour* and *weigh*). Other common exceptions to this rule are: *counterfeit, foreign, forfeit, leisure, reign, seize, sovereign.*

- Think about the meanings of words which sound the same but have different spellings (e.g. *their/there/they're* and *to/too/two*).

Plurals

- **Regular** plurals are formed by simply adding an *s* to the singular word (e.g. *horse–horses; dog–dogs*)

- Words which end with a consonant followed by *y* form the plural by changing the *y* to *ies* (e.g. *baby–babies; lady–ladies*)

- To form the plural of a word ending in *s, x, z, ch, sh* or *ss*, add *es* (e.g. *bus–buses, fox–foxes, church–churches, miss–misses*)

- Most singular words which end with *f* or *fe* change the *f* or *fe* to *ves* to form the plural (e.g. *knife–knives; leaf–leaves; wife–wives*). Common exceptions to this rule are *chief, dwarf, roof* and *safe* which simply add an *s* to form their plural.

- A few words can form their plural either by adding *s* or by changing the final *f* to *ves* (e.g. *hoof; scarf; wharf*).

Check yourself

Spelling (1–2)

1 Which spelling rules do
the following words illustrate?
- **(a)** neighbour (1)
- **(b)** hurried (1)
- **(c)** making (1)
- **(d)** already (1)
- **(e)** deceive (1)
- **(f)** dropped (1)
- **(g)** retrieve (1)
- **(h)** lovely (1)
- **(i)** useful (1)
- **(j)** swimming (1)

*Good spelling is seen as an
important social skill*

2 Check that you know the following spellings by using the
LOOK – COVER – WRITE – CHECK technique:
- **(a)** independent (1)
- **(b)** appropriate (1)
- **(c)** technological (1)
- **(d)** beautiful (1)
- **(e)** dramatically (1)

*Even if you have access to a spell-
checker, don't desert your dictionary!*

3 What are the plural forms of the following words?
- **(a)** baby (1)
- **(b)** church (1)
- **(c)** fox (1)
- **(d)** roof (1)
- **(e)** wharf (1)

1 Spelling rules
   (a) neighbour – if the sound is *ay*, the *i before e* rule does not apply (1)
   (b) hurried – change *y* to *i* before endings (except *ing*) (1)
   (c) making – drop the final *e* before endings which start with a vowel (1)
   (d) already – drop one *l* from *all* before another syllable (1)
   (e) deceive – *e* before *i* after *c* (1)
   (f) dropped – double the final consonant before adding an ending (1)
   (g) retrieve – *i* before *e* except after *c* (1)
   (h) lovely – keep the final *e* if adding an ending which begins with a consonant (1)
   (i) useful – drop one *l* from *full* when adding it to another word (1)
   (j) swimming – double the final consonant if adding an ending beginning with a vowel (1)

Find examples of words which fit these rules in your own writing. You will learn them more easily if you can remember them in a particular sentence that you have used.

2 LOOK – COVER – WRITE – CHECK
   (a) independent (1)
   (b) appropriate (1)
   (c) technological (1)
   (d) beautiful (1)
   (e) dramatically (1)

These may be words that you need to use in various GCSE exams. Make sure that you learn the spellings of technical terms in each of your subjects.

3 Plural forms
   (a) babies (1)
   (b) churches (1)
   (c) foxes (1)
   (d) roofs (1)
   (e) wharfs *or* wharves (1)

TOTAL

Sentences

Basic sentence punctuation requires an upper case (or capital) letter at the start and a full stop at the end. Longer sentences may need commas, semi-colons, colons, exclamation or question marks.

In *Lord of the Flies*, William Golding writes:

> He was old enough, twelve years and a few months, to have lost the prominent tummy of childhood; and not yet old enough for adolescence to have made him awkward.

Because the sentence contains two definite ideas – contrasting childhood and adolescence – they have been separated with a semi-colon. This shows a sophisticated grasp of sentence structure and punctuation. It is better than writing two separate sentences as the ideas are closely linked. The commas in this example are used to separate a descriptive phrase (which adds to the meaning, but is not indispensable) from the main sentence.

The other main use of commas is to separate a list, as in this example from Harper Lee's *To Kill a Mockingbird*:

> Of all days Sunday was the day for formal afternoon visiting: ladies wore corsets, men wore coats, children wore shoes.

This example also shows the most frequent use of the colon, which is to introduce a list.

Question marks must be put at the end of direct questions.
Exclamation marks indicate strong emotions such as anger or astonishment as well as humour. Remember that well-chosen words will convey emotion too, and do not rely on exclamation marks alone to affect your reader's response!

Punctuating speech

Another passage from *Lord of the Flies* illustrates the main rules.

> 'I don't care what they call me,' he said confidentially, 'so long as they don't call me what they used to call me at school.'
>
> Ralph was faintly interested.
>
> 'What was that?'
>
> The fat boy glanced over his shoulder, then leaned towards Ralph.
>
> He whispered.
>
> 'They used to call me "Piggy".'

Note that you should:
- put all the words spoken inside speech marks;
- begin each new piece of speech with a capital letter unless it is the continuation of a sentence (as in Piggy's opening remark);
- place punctuation of the spoken words inside the speech marks (e.g. the comma after 'me' in the first line, and the question mark at the end of Ralph's query);
- use double speech marks inside the normal single speech marks for a title or nickname, as in the last line above.

Apostrophes

These have two functions:
- to show missing letters in abbreviated words such as *wasn't* (was not), *can't* (cannot), *I've* (I have) and so on. The apostrophe is placed where the missing letters would be.
- to show possession (e.g. *the boy's coat*, *the women's partners*).

Remember that *it's* means *it is* (e.g. *it's very hot in here*); *its* means *belonging to it*, as in *the dog chased its ball*.

Punctuation (1–2)

1 Insert two commas and two semi-colons in this sentence from *Turned* by Charlotte Perkins Gilmore (4):

> She sobbed bitterly chokingly despairingly her shoulders heaved and shook convulsively her hands were tight-clenched.

2 Insert the missing punctuation into this passage from *The Darkness Out There* by Penelope Lively (16):

> The door opened Kerry said wherell I put the clippings theres the compost heap down the bottom by the fence and while youre down there could you get some sticks from the wood for kindling theres a good lad

1 In the original the punctuation is:

> She sobbed bitterly, (1) chokingly, (1) despairingly; (1)
> her shoulders heaved and shook convulsively; (1) her
> hands were tight-clenched.

There are no alternatives possible here; the commas separate
a list of adverbs and the semi-colons separate the three parts
of the sentence – which describe the woman's sobbing, then
her shoulders, then her hands.

2 In the original the punctuation is:

> The door opened. (1) Kerry said, (1) '(1)Where'll (2)
> I put the clippings?(1)'
>
> '(1)There's (2) the compost heap down the bottom,
> (1) by the fence. (1) And (1) while you're (1) down
> there could you get some sticks from the wood for
> kindling, (1) there's (1) a good lad (1).'

Note only one mark is given for each pair of speech marks.
Two marks are given in each case for *Where'll* and *There's* as
each requires a capital letter and an apostrophe.

An allowable alternative would be to put a comma after
'fence', a small 'a' for 'and', and another comma after 'there'.

If you start a passage of direct speech with a phrase such
as 'Kerry said', you must put a comma after these words and
before the speech marks – but remember to start the spoken
words with a capital letter. Here is another example from *Salt
on the Snow* by Rukshana Smith:

> Rashmi pointed to the ceiling and Julie
> said, 'Not where, how?'

TOTAL

VOCABULARY AND STYLE (1)

Formal writing

You may well be asked to produce a piece of formal writing in your examination. In formal writing you must choose your words more carefully and precisely than you would if making casual notes or if in conversation with a friend. Consider this sentence from *Birdsong* by Sebastian Faulks:

> **The town side of the boulevard backed on to substantial gardens which were squared off and apportioned with civic precision to the houses they adjoined.**

Note how the writer conveys the impression that this street is inhabited by well-off and important (perhaps even self-important), orderly and conventional people. All of this is done by using words such as 'substantial', 'squared off', 'apportioned', 'civic', 'precision' and 'adjoined'. Not a word is wasted in suggesting the characters of the inhabitants before you have actually met them. Even the use of 'houses' rather than *homes* implies rather cold or unemotional people. Think how little you would be able to speculate about them if the author had simply written, *The houses on the town side of the boulevard had large, neat gardens*. There is nothing 'flashy' about this writing: merely well-chosen words which, together, give a clear viewpoint and invite some speculation.

Narrative

When you are writing narrative, think about structure as well as vocabulary and style. For example, could you achieve a more striking effect by using flashbacks or multiple viewpoints than by writing a straightforward chronological account? Could you use an updated version, in a different setting, of a traditional or well-known story to convey a particular message? While you should always try to be original and fresh in your choice of language, reworking a traditional form is acceptable. It may help you present your ideas effectively. (Look back at pages 29–30 and 33–34 to remind yourself of some possibilities.

Poetry

If you are writing poetry, you are quite likely to use traditional structures and well-known forms. William Blake, for example, contrasts the simple, nursery-rhyme-like form of this verse to

> I was angry with my friend:
> I told my wrath, my wrath did end.
> I was angry with my foe:
> I told it not, my wrath did grow.

highlight a deep and challenging idea in *A Poison Tree*.

In poetry you are using fewer words than in prose, so remember that choosing precise vocabulary is most important. As an example, take this line from Gillian Clarke's poem *Sunday*:

> The cats jump up on windowsills to wash
> And tremble at the starlings.

The word 'tremble' is original but accurate in its picture of cats watching birds. It makes us think, because it is a word which usually suggests fear rather than aggression. Here it applies to both the actions of the aggressors (the cats) and the feelings of the potential victims (the starlings).

Non-fiction texts

You need to be equally precise when you are writing some types of non-fiction. Your personal writing needs to evoke people, places, events and feelings through the vocabulary and imagery you use. Your descriptive or informative writing must be clear, to the point, and sensibly structured if its purpose is to be understood.

Vocabulary and style (1–2)

1 Read this extract from Penelope Lively's *The Darkness Out There*. It describes a girl walking past a place where a German fighter plane had crashed during the war, killing its crew. Comment on the effectiveness of the <u>underlined</u> words, phrases and punctuation (10):

> She kept to the track, walking in the flowers with corn <u>running</u> in the wind between her and the spinney. She thought suddenly of blank-eyed helmeted heads, looking at you from among the branches. She wouldn't go in there for a thousand pounds, not even in bright day like now, with nothing coming out of the <u>dark slab of trees</u> but bird song – blackbirds and thrushes and robins and that. It was a <u>rank</u> place, all <u>whippy</u> saplings and brambles and a gully with a dumped mattress and bedstead and an old fridge. And somewhere, presumably, the crumbling rusty scraps of metal and cloth and <u>...</u> bones?

2 These lines are from *Wil Williams (1861–1910)* by Gillian Clarke.

   (a) What does the description of the stations tell you about what happened to them and why? (3)

   (b) How do the last two lines convey an air of sadness? (3)

> The stations with their cabbage-patches
> and tubbed geraniums are closed
> and the trains' long cries are swallowed
> in the throats of the tunnels.

3 What is particularly effective about these two lines from Bill Bryson's *Notes from a Small Island*? (4) It describes part of a train journey in Wales.

> The towns along the way all had names that sounded like a cat bringing up a hairball: Llywyngwril, Morfa Mawddach, Llandecwyn, Dyffryn Ardudwy.

1 'Running' conveys both an image of the movement of the corn in the wind (1) but also suggests the girl's fear and her own instincts to run past this spooky place (1).
'Dark slab of trees' suggests a threatening presence because of the word 'dark' (1), while 'slab' may make you think of a body at the undertaker's (1).
'Rank' appeals to your sense of smell and emphasises the unpleasantness of the place (1). It is also suggestive of the war (i.e. 'rank' as in ranks of soldiers) (1).
'Whippy' again conveys a sense of movement and threat (1). It also suggests the idea of punishment (1).
'…' is used to make you stop and think (1) and so build up the air of suspense (1).

2 (a) They have been turned into houses (1), with vegetables (1) and flowers (1) growing in the gardens.
  (b) The last two lines convey an air of sadness:
   ● through the reference to swallowing and the throats of tunnels, as in swallowing back tears (1);
   ● the fact that the tunnels are no longer used by trains (1);
   ● the description of the noise once made by the trains as crying (1).

3 The image is effective because it is unexpected (1) and both humorous (1) and slightly disgusting (1); it makes the reader think carefully about the Welsh place-names (1).

All these examples show you how effective single words, images and punctuation can be in your writing. Keep thinking about the **purpose** of what you are writing and the effect you wish to have on your **audience**.

LLYWYNGWRIL	MORFA MAWDDACH
LLANDECWYN	DYFFRYN ARDUDWY

TOTAL

SENTENCE STRUCTURES (1)

Your response to other people's writing, and the style of your own writing, must take account of its intended purpose and its target audience. This means thinking about formality and informality in your use of language. For example, think about how you might aid characterisation by using non-standard forms of English in dialogue in a story. Also important is the extent to which you can show your knowledge of, and control over, a range of different sentence structures.

Note the effective contrast in this extract from Barry Hines' *A Kestrel for a Knave* between informal, non-standard English in the spoken words to the formality and variety in the descriptive writing:

> 'It was a funny feeling though when he'd gone; all quiet, with nobody there, and up to t'knees in tadpoles.'
>
> Silence. The class up to their knees in tadpoles. Mr Farthing allowed them a pause for assimilation. Then, before their involvement could disintegrate into local gossip, he used it to try to inspire an emulator.

Showing a range of techniques

If you can vary the structures of your own writing, you are likely to gain a high grade in your examination. The aim is not only to show your skill in varying sentence structures, but to match them to the needs of the moment. Barry Hines does this by gradually lengthening the sentences. This reflects the tension of the moment, which the teacher tries to capture and maintain.

In writing fiction, then, make the sentence structures play their part in creating mood and conveying atmosphere. Look at this passage from William Golding's *Lord of the Flies*:

> Wave after wave, Ralph followed the rise and fall until something of the remoteness of the sea numbed his brain. Then gradually the almost infinite size of this water forced itself on his attention. This was the divider, the barrier. On the other side of the island, swathed at midday with mirage, defended by the shield of the quiet lagoon, one might dream of rescue; but here, faced by the brute obtuseness of the ocean, the miles of division, one was clamped down, one was helpless, one was condemned, one was –

SENTENCE STRUCTURES (2)

The rhythm of the opening words in the Golding extract reflects the movement of the sea itself. Then the long, unfinished sentence mirrors the difficult nature of the idea with which Ralph is grappling. The mounting panic in his mind is mirrored in the repetitive structure of the closing phrases. Long sentences, carefully used, can be most effective. Combined with the use of the present tense, this technique can give immediacy and forcefulness to writing, especially in a piece of non-fiction. As an example of this, read this extract from *Hong Kong* by Jan Morris:

> I leave my typewriter for a moment, open the sliding glass doors and walk out to the balcony; and away from the hotel's insulated stillness, instantly like the blast of history itself the frantic noise of Hong Kong hits me, the roar of that traffic, the thumping of that jack-hammer, the chatter of a million voices across the city below; and once again the smell of greasy duck and gasoline reaches me headily out of China.

Note the use of semi-colons by both William Golding and Jan Morris. This adds to the effects achieved by both writers in building sweeping sentences which carry the reader along on a flood of ideas and descriptive details.

Another way of achieving immediacy is by using 'ungrammatical' sentences. For example, this is how Dylan Thomas begins *The Outing: A Story*:

> If you can call it a story. There's no real beginning or end and there's very little in the middle.

Sentence structures (1–2)

1 Join the following sentences into one (4):

> He was carrying a foolish wooden stick.
> The boar was only five yards away.
> He flung the stick.
> He saw it hit the great snout.
> It hung there for a moment.

2 Comment on the effects achieved by the sentence structures in this extract from *By Desert Ways to Baghdad* by Louisa Jebb (6):

> Last night we were dirty, isolated, and free, tonight we are clean, sociable and trammelled.
>
> Last night the setting sun's final message written in flaming signs of gold was burnt into us, and the starry heights carried our thoughts heavenward and made them free as ourselves. Tonight the sunset passed all unheeded and we gaze, as we retire from the busy rush of the trivial day, at a never-ending, twisting, twirling pattern on the four walls that imprison us, oppressed by the confining ceiling of our room in the Damascus Palace Hotel.

3 Read this extract from Blake Morrison's *And when did you last see your father?*, in which he describes his father's death from cancer. How do the sentence structures contribute to the feelings he conveys? Think about the grammar and the stylistic features used. (10)

> Midwinter half-light. The hardest frost of the year, and everything has ground to a halt, the ponds frozen, the trees under arrest, the canal locks locked. The sun can do nothing about this. It lies all day on its bed of hills, then sinks red-faced behind Pendle. It can't get up. It can't get up.

1 The example is taken from William Golding's *Lord of the Flies*, where the sentence actually reads:

> With the boar only five yards away, he flung the foolish wooden stick that he carried, saw it hit the great snout and hang there for a moment.

You are unlikely to have come up with precisely this, but award youself 1 mark for each successful join in the sentences.

2 The opening sentence uses repetition of structure (1) to highlight the contrast between last night and tonight (1). The other two sentences develop this technique (1) by expanding details about last night and tonight into one sentence each (1). The three sentences gradually become longer (1), which reflects the writer's sense of frustration at being 'imprisoned' within the decorative fussiness of the hotel room (1).
Always look for structural patterns and repeats such as this in the work of other writers. Think about how you might use them in your own writing. If you are describing contrasts of any kind, repetitive sentence structures in which you change crucial details are highly effective in drawing a reader's attention to the ideas you wish to convey.

3 The first sentence is 'ungrammatical' (1) and gains your attention by making a bare statement about the setting (1). The repetition in the second sentence (1), together with the extended metaphor (1) and the pun on 'lock' (1), emphasises the severity of the weather (1). The personification of the sun (1) reflects the writer's own feelings of helplessness (1). The repetition of the final sentences (1) makes the reader aware that the description has really been about the writer's father as much as the weather (1).

TOTAL

When you plan your own writing, you must have an overview of the whole text – not only its content, but how it moves from the beginning to the end in a way which will engage readers.

When you have finished a piece of writing, you must check and revise it to ensure that the overall structure and effect is what you intended. Careful planning will help greatly. This means thinking about the content of different sections of the text (such as paragraphs), the progress from one section to another, and the beginning and end in particular.

Paragraphs

These organise meaning and make your text accessible to the reader. A paragraph will usually be one or more sentences which are connected by:

- *topic or subject* – perhaps a character or setting in a story, or one aspect of the idea or argument in a non-fiction text;
- *narrative or chronological sequence* (e.g. the stages of a journey made by a character in a story or the order of instructions for assembling a piece of furniture);
- *an argument or approach* (e.g. reasons why you do or don't believe in ghosts in a piece of writing about the supernatural).

Use paragraphs flexibly. They do not have to be so many lines or so many sentences long. Variety in paragraph length – just as in sentence structures – can contribute to the tone or atmosphere you are trying to create. Look at the extract from *Examination Day* by Henry Slesar (overleaf). A boy in a future society is about to undergo an intelligence test to decide if he is allowed to survive or not. The tension is created by each event being in a separate paragraph.

Use paragraphs flexibly.

A concealed loudspeaker crackled and called off the first name.

Dickie saw a boy leave his father's side reluctantly and walk slowly towards the door.

At five minutes of eleven, they called the name of Jordan.

'Good luck, son,' his father said, without looking at him. 'I'll call for you when the test is over.'

Beginnings and endings

Opening paragraphs need to grab your reader's attention. Use them to state an idea boldly, to introduce a memorable character, to start a dialogue which sets up a conflict, or to intrigue your reader with something unusual. This is how Margaret Atwood starts *The Big Man*:

> Julie broke up with Connor in the middle of a swamp.

Endings need plenty of thought as well. You can do various things with an ending. You might neatly round off a story, as Penelope Lively does in *The Darkness Out There*:

> She walked behind him, through a world grown unreliable, in which flowers sparkle and birds sing but everything is not as it appears, oh no.

Or you can try the more risky, but often effective, technique of leaving the reader wondering and wanting more. This is how Charlotte Perkins Gilman ends *Turned*:

> He looked from one to the other dumbly.
> And the woman who had been his wife asked quietly:
> 'What have you to say to us?'

It would be disastrous to leave your reader high and dry in a piece of non-fiction writing, especially if it is instructional in any way. Once again, remember to test your approach against the demands of **purpose** and **audience**.

Structuring whole texts (1–2)

1 Identify the kind of writing for which each of the following might be a suitable beginning (5), and explain why (5):

> **(i)** The body was found, the dagger planted deep in its back, in the windowless, locked drawing-room, with the key jammed in the key-hole on the inside.
>
> **(ii)** 'Oh Joe', she sighed, 'we're always going to be so happy!'
>
> **(iii)** Before you start, make sure that you have identified all the fittings and that the necessary tools are to hand.
>
> **(iv)** Do you really believe that foxes enjoy being torn apart by a pack of hounds?
>
> **(v)** I hadn't expected the Bishop to be wearing a dress, fishnet tights and a lopsided grin when he opened the door.

2 The following are actual endings from books. What kind of book do you think each is, and why? (10)

> **(i)** 'I've had enough of Nakhodka,' Wanda said. Her teeth were chattering. 'It's a hell of a place. What's more I've had enough of Siberia, and we've all had enough of Mischa, and I'm fed up with your damn maps. I want to go home.' So we did.
>
> **(ii)** I signalled the bus-driver and he stopped the bus for me right outside the cottage, and I flew down the steps of the bus straight into the arms of the waiting mother.
>
> **(iii)** When he arrived home there was no one in. He buried the hawk in the field just behind the shed; went in, and went to bed.
>
> **(iv)** As scientists and humanists doctors will be needed to help to provide the answers, a task – to return to George Eliot – that will certainly 'call forth the highest intellectual strain'.
>
> **(v)** The photograph was still there. He was for a moment surprised that Dalgleish hadn't taken it. But then he remembered. It didn't matter. There would be no trial now, no exhibits, no need to produce it as evidence in court. It wasn't needed any more. It was of no importance. He left it on the table and, turning to join Kate, walked with her in silence to the car.

1 **(i)** A detective/whodunnit/mystery story (1) which makes you want to know how the crime was committed (1).

(ii) A romance (1) which might be serious or not/happy or not – you want to know more about the characters (1).

(iii) A set of instructions (1) which ensures that the reader is properly prepared for the task (1).

(iv) A piece of argumentative writing/polemic (see page 104) (1) which makes you question your own beliefs/attitudes (1).

(v) Probably a humorous story, possibly a mystery (1), which is so bizarre in the picture it conjures up that you want to know more (1).

You will probably write more subtly than in these examples, but they illustrate how easily you can set up expectations in your readers.

2 **(i)** A travel book (*The Big Red Train Ride* by Eric Newby) (1) – the clues are in the place-names and the reference to going home (1).

(ii) An autobiography (Roald Dahl's *Going Solo*) (1) – the clue is the reference to mother (1).
This is less obvious than the previous example – it could conceivably have been the end of a novel or short story.

(iii) A novel (*A Kestrel for a Knave* by Barry Hines) (1) – the clue is that it is clearly part of a narrative (1).

(iv) A non-fiction text (Alan Norton, *Drugs, Science and Society*) (1) – the clue is in the references to scientists/doctors and the fact that this is clearly the end of presenting an argument of some sort (1).

(v) A detective story (*Original Sin* by P. D. James) (1) – the clue is in the references to trial, exhibits and court (1).

TOTAL

Your written work cannot achieve its full effect on the reader (especially if that reader is an examiner) unless you present it neatly and clearly. Depending on the kind or genre of writing it is, it may also be helpful to use a range of suitable presentational devices to break up the text.

Handwriting

However much you like to use computers for coursework, you will have to handwrite your examination papers. Try to develop handwriting which uses CLUES:

- **C**onsistently shaped and joined letters
- **L**etters – clear distinction between upper (capital) and lower (small) case
- **U**pright, or at least always leans in the same direction
- **E**venly spaced
- **S**ensible size – neither too cramped nor too spread out.

Consider what you use to write with – the correct pen for you (in terms of diameter, balance, weight and so on) will improve both the speed and quality of your handwriting.

Breaking up the text

If writing prose fiction, remember to use paragraphs (page 85). You might also use chapter headings in a longer story. You could use titles in a sequence of poems, which may be broken up into stanzas (or verses). Scripts for media such as stage, radio, film or television need to follow appropriate layout conventions regarding stage/camera directions, set details and so on.

If you are writing non-fiction, remember that you can use a range of devices – including titles, underlinings, different margin sizes/ indentations, headings and subheadings, frames, bullet points and numbered instructions. All of these can be done by hand in an examination, where appropriate.

Titles, charts and diagrams may also make your meaning clearer, but may be less easy to produce without IT. Do not try to use a range of colours on your examination paper, as this may cause confusion for markers and checkers at a later stage. In fact, many examination boards instruct you to use only blue or black ink in their answer books.

Editing and proofreading

The final aspect of presentation is the last set of checks that you carry out in an examination. **Editing** means looking back over the work you have written and asking yourself the following questions:

- Have I adopted the best tone/approach for the target audience, using a range of appropriate language and grammatical constructions?
- Have I achieved my purpose in the overall effect of the piece?
- Have I made the best choice of content in respect of audience and purpose?
- Is the structure and presentation of the piece logical, coherent and helpful?
- Is the piece easily understood and attractive to look at?

Proofreading means checking:

- Spelling
- Punctuation
- Grammar

Good spelling is essential as an important social skill.

Don't worry about making alterations or corrections in your work. If you do it neatly, the examiner will be impressed that you have checked your work thoroughly in the first place, and that you have been able to identify and correct errors.

Presenting written work (1–2)

1 An examination question gives you a text on the subject of under-age drinking and asks you to re-present it in an appropriate, attractive style for teenagers. Suggest six presentational devices you could employ in an examination answer, and explain the usefulness of each (12).

2 What are the five aspects of editing you should know and use in an examination? (5)

3 What are the three aspects of proofreading you should know and use in an examination? (3)

1 Presentational devices:
   (i) Title (1) to attract the reader's interest (1).
   (ii) Sub-headings (1) help to make the structure of the argument clear to readers (1).
   (iii) Bullet points (1) can clarify lists and/or emphasise important points (1).
   (iv) Diagrams (1) give an attractive appearance/appeal to less keen readers (1).
   (v) Graphs/charts/tables (1) can make statistical information/figures easier to take in (1).
   (vi) Framing and/or writing in columns (1) can break up an otherwise large area of text and make it more accessible (1).

2 Five aspects of editing:
   (i) Is the tone/approach right for the target audience? (Have I used a range of appropriate language and grammatical constructions?) (1)
   (ii) Have I achieved my purpose in the overall effect of the piece? (1)
   (iii) Have I made the best choice of content in respect of audience and purpose? (1)
   (iv) Is the structure and presentation of the piece logical, coherent and helpful? (1)
   (v) Is the piece easily understood and attractive to look at? (1)

3 Three aspects of proofreading:
   ● Spelling (1)
   ● Punctuation (1)
   ● Grammar (1)

TOTAL

Writing to explore, imagine and entertain

The **purpose** of some writing you will be asked to do in your exam is to *explore*, *imagine* or *entertain*. This is most likely to be a piece of narrative or descriptive prose. It may be based on your own experience or be wholly or partly imagined. Your first planning issue is to think about the **audience** for your writing. If it is a story for a young child, the structure may follow conventions such as 'Once upon a time ...' and '... they all lived happily ever after', while the characters may be simply 'bad' or 'good'. Even so, you must plan features such as **plot**, **characters**, **setting**, **ideas**, **structure** and **style** carefully. Make sure they work together to serve your purpose and please your audience. If writing for a more mature reader, you may think about using techniques such as **flashback** or **multiple viewpoints**.

Plot

Concentrate on exploring one event, character or issue in detail, depending on your purpose; you will not have time for too much complication when writing in the exam. Even if you are writing fantasy, you must make it believable for your intended audience.

Characters

Concentrate on a few, well-described, different characters and use a wide range of descriptive vocabulary. Show character through speech and action. When Marcus, in *The Go-Between* by L. P. Hartley, says

> 'Leo, you mustn't come down to breakfast in your slippers. It's the sort of thing that bank clerks do.'

the reader gains an immediate idea of his background and attitudes.

Similarly, when Napoleon in George Orwell's *Animal Farm* urinates on Snowball's plans for the windmill, this action characterises him far more effectively than any amount of description.

WRITING (2)

Setting

Plan the place, the season, the time of day and the weather: all can create the desired effect on your audience. As when describing character, this is an opportunity for you to show the range of your vocabulary. Kingshaw's fear in Susan Hill's *I'm the King of the Castle* is emphasised here by the word 'spearing' and by the claustrophobic setting:

> The sun was spearing, now and again, through the network of leaves, and rippling over the tree trunks like water. But mostly, the leaves were too thick to let much light in. It was very close, too, now that they were well into the wood, the air that he took in at his mouth felt warm, and somehow thicker than normal air.

Ideas

Remember your purpose: is there a 'message'? There will be a greater effect on readers if there is, but don't tack it crudely on the end: it should be implicit in the narrative, largely through the characters you create, the situations you put them into and the development of the plot.

Structure

Who tells the story? Is it chronological, or are there flashbacks? What makes the beginning seize the reader's attention? What makes the end unforgettable? Plan all of this, but remember limitations of time in the exam.

Style

Show what you can do:
● detailed and original descriptions which create a sense of place and atmosphere in your readers' minds
● sentences and paragraphs which vary in length and structure to change the pace of the story
● realistic dialogue to bring the characters to life.

Writing (1–2)

1 Apart from the purpose of your writing, what is the most important overall consideration when planning a narrative? (1)

2 What are the six features you should think about when planning a narrative? (6)

3 What three ways are there of conveying character in a narrative? (3)

4 Name four aspects of setting which could affect a reader's response to a narrative. (4)

5 For each of the following identify why it is an effective opening to a narrative, and suggest what kind of narrative it is likely to be. (6)

(a)

> He had never seen such a gruesome sight – the pale light of the moon shone wanly on the twisted features of the dead man.

(b)

> 'Oh Emma,' laughed John, 'we're going to have such a lovely day!'

(c)

> I realised the autobutler was malfunctioning when I saw my breakfast plastered on the ceiling and my trousers hanging from the lampshade.

1 The audience for which you are writing (1).

2 Character (1), setting (1), ideas (1), structure (1) and style (1).

3 Through description (1), speech (1) and action (1).
It is a good idea to try to use all of these ways in your writing, so that one paragraph about a character might include some description, some speech and some action. For example:

> The large, ruddy-faced man barged through the door, slammed on it with one of his huge fists and shouted aggressively, 'Does anyone here want me?'

4 Place (1), season (1), time (1) and weather (1).
Once again, you will often combine these features in your writing so that if you wanted to set the scene for a rather sad story you might begin:

> The cemetery, in late October, was a miserable place to begin with. Today, with darkness already falling at only three o'clock, and heavy rain lashing against the headstones, it seemed that winter had arrived with a vengeance.

5 (a) This is an effective opening because you wonder who the dead man is, why he is dead and so on (1). It is probably the opening of a murder mystery or a detective story (1).

   (b) This is an effective opening because the reader wonders whether Emma and Jack really will have a lovely day or not (1). It is probably the opening of a romantic story, but not necessarily one with a happy ending (1).

   (c) This is an effective opening because it is amusing and intriguing (1). It is probably the opening of a humorous science-fiction story (1).

In the exam, you won't have time to plan a whole story in great detail. Once you have your basic idea, it is worth working on your opening and closing paragraphs.

TOTAL

Writing to inform, explain and describe

This kind of writing is the response to exam questions which ask you to:

- **inform** someone about an event, or how to do something
- **explain** how something works or how to get from one place to another
- **describe** what something feels or looks like.

Although you may need to use some imagination, you can often base responses on your own experiences and observations. The exam paper may give you stimulus material to help you with the content – it is your writing skills which will be tested, not your general knowledge.

Audience and purpose

Take particular notice of the audience and purpose you are given. For example, the purpose of a task might be to write to a visitor to your school, informing him or her of the arrangements, explaining how to get there and describing what facilities are available. This would be a polite and formal piece of work, probably written in quite plain, functional language. You might use bullet points or sketches to clarify certain information.

Your response to a task which asked you to write about an early memory, explaining how it has affected you, would be quite different. In this case, your style would be less formal, allowing you to use a more imaginative range of vocabulary and sentence structures.

Remember that the needs of a given audience will help you decide on the content and tone of your writing. If you were asked to write an informative piece about video recorders, explaining how to use them and describing the benefits they can bring, the nature of your final text would depend, for example, on whether it was written for a ten year old or a mature adult.

Early memories can be very vivid

WRITING (4)

Personal and impersonal

An important decision you have to make in planning informative, explanatory or descriptive writing is how personal it should be. Should thoughts and feelings come into it, or should it be factual and to the point?

Once again, this comes back to purpose and audience. It would probably not be appropiate to include anything other than information in the letter to a school visitor, mentioned previously – but if you already knew the visitor well, then you would approach the task quite differently. Similarly, with the piece about video recorders: if your purpose was to inform and explain to a child, your writing would be straightforward and to the point. If, on the other hand, you wanted to amuse an older person by making out that video recorders are extremely difficult to tame, then your approach would be more imaginative and free.

This choice is most often apparent in writing which is largely descriptive rather than informative or explanatory. It is possible, but not easy, to write impersonal, neutral descriptions – and they are often very dull.

This description from Bill Bryson's *Notes From a Small Island* gives plenty of information and explanation, but is made more interesting because of his obvious anger which comes through in the choice of language:

> A couple of miles beyond Kimmeridge, at the far side of a monumentally steep hill, stands the little lost village of Tyneham, or what's left of it. In 1943, the Army ordered Tyneham's inhabitants to leave for a bit as they wanted to practise lobbing shells into the surrounding hillsides. The villagers were solemnly promised that once Hitler was licked, they could all come back. Fifty-one years later they were still waiting. Forgive my disrespectful tone, but this seems to me disgraceful…

Writing (3–4)

1 (a) Explain the chief differences between impersonal and personal styles of writing (6).

(b) Describe when it would be appropriate to use each of these styles in your writing (6).

2 What different effects are achieved, and how, by these two passages? (8)

The first evening of her stay in Kuching we went for a row on the river, and the sunset behind matang was, as she said, a revelation. That land of forests, mountains and water, the wonderful effect of sunshine and cloud, the sudden storms, the soft mists at evening, the perfumed air brought through miles and miles of forest by the night breezes, were an endless source of delight to her. Sometimes as we sat on our verandah in the evening after dinner, a sweet, strange perfume wafted from forest lands beyond, across the river, floated through our house – 'The scent of unknown flowers,' Miss North would say...

(from *Good Morning and Good Night* by Lady Margaret Brooke)

The problems that climate and landscape features pose are not confined to one part of the world. Cattle ranchers and arable farmers in many countries are experiencing equally severe difficulties. The farmers in the outback of Australia, for example, face desiccation of their grazing land, whilst huge areas of the continent of Africa face the prospect of encroaching deserts. It is thought that two-thirds of the world's countries are affected to some extent, though the problem was only brought to world attention by the catastrophic droughts of the Sahel region in the 1970s.

(from *16–19 Core Geography* by Naish and Warn)

1 (a) Impersonal writing is largely factual and/or informative
(1) and is written in formal (1) and fairly plain language
(1). Personal writing may still be factual but will include
more opinions and ideas (1) and a wider range of
imaginative or expressive vocabulary (1); overall, it will
be less formal than impersonal writing (1).

(b) An impersonal style should be used when writing to an
unknown audience (1), and in situations where
politeness (1) and clarity (1) are important. A personal
style is appropriate when the writing is for a known
audience (1) which is comfortable with informality (1)
and where humour or imagination, or the conveying
of some other feeling, is more important than
pure information (1).

Although particularly relevant here, this distinction applies to
other styles of writing in addition to informing, explaining and
describing. It is worth thinking about whenever you are
deciding on the approach to a particular writing task.

2 Both passages are informing/explaining/describing, but the
first is written in a personal, literary style (1) with long
sentences (1) and many references to the senses (1). The
second is more impersonal (1) and conveys information rather
than sensation (1). The piece is logically structured (1), but
the tone is not entirely neutral (1) as is shown by the use of
words such as 'severe' and 'catastrophic' (1).

The second passage shows again that, even in a textbook, it is
very difficult to write in this style without judgements or
feelings emerging. Don't worry about this. However, be aware
of it in your own writing so that, when formality or
impersonality is required, you can control the other aspects of
your style.

TOTAL

Writing to argue, persuade and instruct

This group includes writing in which the purpose is to present opinions or arguments in ways which will persuade the audience. This has to be done by:
- changing the reader's views if they differ from your own;
- strengthening the reader's views if they are similar to your own;
- suggesting why it is good to hold particular views.

Within this category, typical exam tasks might be to:
- argue about an aspect of modern life, such as making the case for birth control or against nuclear power;
- examine a common problem and suggest the most sensible approach to it – such as overcoming famine in Africa;
- prepare advice for young children on how to avoid dangers in the home.

To shock or not to shock?

By its nature, this kind of writing tends to involve strong emotions and deeply-held beliefs. Sometimes, shocking readers with the strength of your views is a good way of gaining attention before you try to persuade or instruct them. However, strong feelings can get in the way of presenting a case logically and clearly. Readers may switch off if they feel they are being preached at, or if your writing is not clear. The best arguments persuade through instruction – that is, they present evidence to people which makes them think about, and perhaps change, their views.

Shocking your reader

WRITING (6)

Keeping cool

Going to the other extreme and deliberately avoiding high emotion can be an effective way of engaging your reader's sympathies. This is how George Orwell describes a hanging in a Burmese jail:

> There was a clanking noise, and then dead silence. The prisoner had vanished, and the rope was twisting on itself. I let go of the dog, and it galloped immediately to the back of the gallows; but when it got there it stopped short, barked, and then retreated into a corner of the yard, where it stood among the weeds, looking timorously out at us. We went round the gallows to inspect the prisoner's body. He was dangling with his toes pointed straight downwards, very slowly revolving, as dead as a stone.

This is an almost detached description of a terrible event. The writer's feelings of revulsion are conveyed to us not through violent outbursts but through the detail of the dog and its reactions.

Points of view

Willingness to admit different points of view in your writing can strengthen an argument, since it makes you appear reasonable rather than fanatical. It also shows your ability to collect and cross-reference a range of ideas.

Stylistic devices

Depending on the purpose and audience for your writing, and the form it is taking, think about using:
- presentational devices such as headings and sub-headings, and bullet points;
- charts and graphs or other evidence to support your views (but don't go mad with statistics);
- carefully chosen vocabulary and imagery which will create a picture in the reader's mind (such as in Orwell's final sentence above);
- direct appeals and questions to the reader, such as 'Do you think this is right?' Then you should go on to answer the appeal on the reader's behalf in a way which advances your case.

Writing (5–6)

1 Explain how this writer (Vicente Blasco Ibanez in *Blood and Sand*) uses the description of the animal's death at the end of a bullfight to make a statement against the sport. Think about the contrast between the two sentences (2), pick examples of powerful language (4) and say what the overall effect of the passage is (2).

> The bull was still carried along by the impetus of its charge, with the red handle of the sword standing out from its broad neck, where it was buried up to the hilt. Suddenly it stopped short in its career, rocked forward with a painful curtsying motion; its forelegs doubled under it, its head sank lower till the bellowing muzzle touched the sand, and it subsided full length in the convulsions of its final agony ...

2 How successfully does this newspaper report on damage to the countryside make a powerful argument for its case through expressing strong opinions? Pick out the words and phrases which contribute to the effect (12).

> 'More tears have been shed, more hands wrung, more mud thrown over the destruction of rural England than over any other tragedy since World War II,' said Richard Girling in The Sunday Times. 'Yet still the machines roll on.' Protecting the countryside would be easy if the threat were from 'a single blow of the axe'. Instead, it faces 'death by a thousand cuts'. Planners, developers, politicians, supermarkets and farmers have all 'hacked away at rural England until, in many places, not an echo of it remains beyond the mockery of suburban street names with their flowerless Meadows and treeless Woods'.

1 The writer takes a fairly matter-of-fact approach (1) in the first sentence, but then chooses words and phrases which make the dying bull seem pitiable (1) – such as 'painful curtsying motion' (1), 'bellowing' (1), 'convulsions' (1), and 'agony' (1). The description conjures up a strong visual image (1) of the huge animal collapsing into an undignified heap (1).

The writer may not have intended this to be an anti-bullfighting statement, but it is a good example of how a fairly restrained description can be used to evoke a particular mood. If you were writing an attack on bullfighting, you would probably want to assemble some statistics about deaths and injuries to both bulls and bullfighters, and other factual material, but a description such as this could be an effective opening.

2 The piece is successful because the force of the language makes it hard to ignore the argument (1). Words and phrases such as 'tears' (1), 'hands wrung' (1), 'destruction' (1), 'tragedy' (1), 'single blow of the axe' (1), 'death by a thousand cuts' (1), 'hacked away' (1), 'hideous mockery' (1) all contribute to an overall image of violence (1) and a contempt (1) for hideous modern suburbia (1).

Powerful one-sided arguments are known as 'polemic' – and it can be very effective if used sparingly. Remember, though, that a balanced argument may be a better way of showing your writing skills, particularly your ability to handle different points of view.

TOTAL

Writing to analyse, review and comment

This is the kind of writing you need to produce if an exam question asks you to:

- identify and describe the particular qualities of a person, place, event, book, advertisement, etc. – this is **analysing**;
- describe and explain what those particular qualities tell you about the person, place, book or advertisement – this is **reviewing**;
- explain and identify your reaction to, and the significance of, the person, place, book or advertisement – this is **commenting**.

You are most likely to use this kind of writing when you respond to texts, in personal writing, such as a piece of autobiography or an account of work experience, or in writing about social or historical issues.

Purpose and audience

These are key concepts, whatever kind of writing you are doing. In this case, your purpose might range from amusing a friend with an account of something you did as a young child, to impressing a magazine editor with your thoughts on the latest novel by a famous author.

Language and structure

Your choice of vocabulary needs to be very precise and the structure of your writing should develop in a coherent way. An example is this description by Bill Bryson of the development of the Kodak Company:

From the outset Eastman developed three crucial strategies that have been the hallmarks of virtually every successful consumer-goods company since. First, he went for the mass market, reasoning that it was better to make a little money each from a lot of people rather than a lot of money from a few. He also showed a tireless, obsessive dedication to making his products better and cheaper.

BILL BRYSON
Notes FROM A
SMALL ISLAND

Note how Bill Bryson uses words like 'crucial', 'strategies', 'hallmarks', 'consumer-goods', 'mass market' to give authority to the writing. Also note how 'obsessive' and 'dedication' create a quick and convincing pen-portrait of George Eastman, the founder of the Kodak Company. The structure is held together by words such as 'from the outset', 'first' and 'also'. The reversal of 'a little...a lot' and 'a lot...a few' is a neat structural feature.

Personal and impersonal analytical writing

Analytical writing is often **impersonal** and written in the third person ('he/she'). Even when written in the first person ('I') the language and style can be objective and logical. For example, the following extract from an essay on the freedom of the press:

> However, I think that the issue goes far beyond the invasion of the privacy of a handful of people. The public has a right to know what is going on, and the proposed curbs would cut information down to a minimum.

The word 'however', and similar words such as 'nevertheless', 'therefore' and 'although' are useful in constructing this kind of writing.

Personal analytical writing may involve deep emotions. Even so, vocabulary and sentence structures need to be carefully planned if the writer is to communicate effectively with the reader. This is the end of an account of a girl meeting her father, whom she has not seen for a long time:

> I stepped down onto the platform and with trembling, uneasy steps I made my way through the crowds to this man. He saw me, came and took my cases, but then put them down. This man had a large grin on his face and his arms were open; he leant over and hugged me. All the thoughts I had experienced on the train left my head. This man was my father.

The vocabulary – apart from 'trembling, uneasy' – is plain but effective; the repetition of 'this man' hints at uncertainty. Then the short final sentence, revealing 'this man' to be the father, contrasts dramatically with the previous longer sentences.

Writing (7–8)

1 What are the two key concepts in planning any piece of writing? (2)

2 List four linking words which may be particularly useful in constructing a coherent, logical analysis. (4)

3 The following is from *Going Solo* by Roald Dahl.
   (a) Pick out four words which are used especially effectively (4).
   (b) Pick out two structural features which make the passage a successful piece of analytical writing (2).

> A life is made up of a great number of small incidents and a small number of great ones. An autobiography must therefore, unless it is to become tedious, be extremely selective, discarding all the inconsequential incidents in one's life and concentrating upon those that have remained vivid in the memory.

4 Read the following passage. It is from *Notes from a Small Island* by Bill Bryson.
   (a) Identify four words which help in linking the sentences into a clear, logical analysis (4).
   (b) Select four words which give the passage authority: one technical term to do with business and three to do with building (4).

> As the nineteenth century progressed and small companies grew into mighty corporations, the new breed of magnates required increasingly grand and imposing headquarters. Fortunately, their need for office space coincided with the development of a radical type of building: the skyscraper. Before the 1880s, buildings of more than eight or nine storeys were impracticable. Such a structure, made of brick, would require so much support as to preclude openings for windows and doors on the lower floors. However, a number of small innovations and one large one suddenly made skyscrapers a practical proposition. The large innovation was curtain-walling, a cladding of non-weight-bearing materials hung on a steel skeleton, which made tall buildings much easier to build.

1 Purpose (1) and audience (1).

2 However (1); nevertheless (1); therefore (1); although (1).
Look out for pieces of writing in which these words are used, and note how they link sentences or paragraphs. If you use them skilfully, you are bound to be explaining ideas to your audience in a clear way, and the structure of your writing will therefore serve its purpose.

3 (a) Four words used precisely and effectively are: 'tedious' (1), 'selective' (1), 'inconsequential' (1) and 'vivid' (1).
'Tedious' is a better choice than 'boring'; 'selective' admits that an autobiography does not give the whole picture; 'inconsequential' is another word for 'small' or 'unimportant' but shows a wide vocabulary; 'vivid' is a more engaging word than, say, 'clear'.

(b) Two structural features worthy of comment are the use of 'therefore' (1) and the reversal in the first sentence of 'great...small' and 'small...great' (1).
See the comment in 2 above about the use of words such as 'therefore'. Reversing pairs of words is a common and effective device, which always catches the reader's attention. Similar devices, such as repeating a phrase almost exactly with a small but significant change, are equally effective.

4 (a) The four significant linking words are: 'As ...' (1); 'Fortunately ...' (1); 'Before ...' (1); 'However ...' (1).
Reread the passage and see how it is these words which lead you carefully through the writer's material. Then you will understand how one aspect of Bill Bryson's argument relates to another.

(b) The following could be seen to give the passage technical authority: 'magnates' (1), the term from business; 'curtain-walling' (1), 'cladding' (1) and 'non-weight-bearing' (1), the building terms.

TOTAL

ORGANISING TALK (1)

When taking part in a speaking and listening activity which is being assessed for your exam, you need to concentrate on three things:

● your **topic** (what you are going to say);
● your **purpose** (what you want to achieve by saying it);
● your **audience** (who you are talking to).

Thinking about this will help you decide how **formal** or **informal** your words should be. It will also help to decide whether you should rely just on the power of speech or whether you should use visual aids such as diagrams or pictures. Formal speech means avoiding slang and incomplete sentences; this is particularly important – and courteous – if you are speaking to an unknown audience.

General techniques you should use in all oral work include:

● speaking clearly and firmly to make sure that everyone can hear you;
● varying the tone, pitch and pace of your voice to keep your audience's attention;

and in groupwork particularly:

● being polite but insistent in making your points heard;
● being prepared to give way to someone else who wishes to speak.

Individual and pair work

On your own, or with a partner, you will probably need to show skills such as **describing** or **narrating**. For example, if you are talking about, or comparing, personal experiences. You may also need to **explore**, **analyse** or **imagine**. For example, if working on the meaning of a text you have not seen before, or preparing a role play.

Group work

In a group discussion, your function is to be part of a team which has a task to complete together, but make sure your own contributions show how well you can **explain**, **argue** and **persuade**.

Explaining means using your knowledge and experience to put across your own point of view. Don't be afraid to challenge the audience with new ideas. Others will concentrate:
● if your choice of language is interesting;
● if you present what you say in an organised way;
● if, in other words, you remember topic and audience.

Arguing and **persuading** means conveying a point of view, which may not be shared by others. It does not mean losing your temper, even if you believe passionately in what you say and no one else does. It means using techniques such as:
● questions (not necessarily expecting answers);
● repetition of key words, phrases, and ideas.

It also means convincing others that your point of view is right by:
● varying the structure and length of your sentences for dramatic effect;
● using powerful and vivid vocabulary;
● using humour (often more powerful than anger);
● using evidence to support what you say;
● in other words, achieving your purpose.

Chairing a group discussion

In this role you will have fewer opportunities to put forward your own ideas and points of view. Instead, you should:
● introduce the topic so that all members of the group understand what they are expected to achieve;
● sometimes ask questions, seek clarification and occasionally summarise what has been said so that all members of the group understand what is going on;
● keep the group on task, and draw anyone who does not seem involved into the discussion;
● summarise the discussion at the end and check that the group agrees that it has achieved its purpose.

Organising talk (1–2)

1 What four general issues do you need to consider when preparing for an oral assessment? (4)

2 What four general speaking techniques should you remember? (4)

3 Comment on the successful techniques used in this contribution to a group discussion on capital punishment (7):

> I don't believe in capital punishment, because I've read a lot about it. I don't think revenge is right, and there have been examples of the wrong person being hung, like Timothy Evans. How would you feel if that was someone you knew? Revenge is wrong, and pointless. Most murders are one-offs committed within the family.

4 What are the main functions of the Chair in a discussion group? (5)

1 Topic (1), purpose (1) and audience (1); whether it is a formal or informal occasion (1).

2 Speak clearly and firmly/audibly (1); vary tone, pitch and pace to keep attention (1); be polite but insistent if you wish to be heard (1); allow others to speak (1).
   Think also about the aspects of body language described on pages 113–114: these are as important when you are speaking as when you are listening. It is very difficult to use the four techniques listed here effectively if you are covering your mouth, or fidgeting, or standing/sitting in a posture which suggests lack of interest. Eye-contact with your audience, and an awareness of appropriate facial expressions, is crucial if you want to command its attention.

3 The speaker:
   ● explains clearly why s/he holds this point of view (1);
   ● describes in more detail why s/he feels that way and gives an example in support (1);
   ● argues effectively by using a rhetorical question (1);
   ● repeats the word 'revenge' (1);
   ● persuades by varying sentence length (1);
   ● uses a range of vocabulary (1);
   ● refers to evidence at the end (1).

4 The Chair's functions are to:
   ● introduce the topic (1);
   ● question, clarify and summarise (1);
   ● keep the group on task (1);
   ● involve everyone in the discussion (1);
   ● summarise at the end (1).
   If you do not take an active part as Chair, it will be very difficult for you to gain marks towards your Speaking and Listening grade.

TOTAL

Active listening means showing that you are listening with interest and understanding. Although listening goes on inside your head, you can show that you are actively involved by:

- giving appropriate non-verbal signals – in other words, your body language;
- giving appropriate verbal signals, such as an occasional 'Really?' or 'Uh-huh' or a similar short phrase;
- responding appropriately when you have a chance to speak.

Body language

This is important both in speaking and listening, and the same techniques apply in both situations:

- *Posture*: sit or stand in an alert way, not slumped with hands in pockets!
- *Facial expressions*: generally, smiles encourage and frowns discourage, but match your expression to what is being said.
- *Gestures and movements*: nods or shakes of the head can be encouraging, but nail biting or fiddling with a pen suggests that you are not involved.
- *Eye-contact*: this is crucial both as a speaker and a listener to maintain interest and concentration.
- *Arm position*: your arms should be relaxed, not tightly folded, to suggest you are listening with an open mind.

Body language can tell you a lot about your listener's attitude.

ACTIVE LISTENING (2)

Hearing and understanding

You need to do more than just show you are listening. You need to hear what is being said, and understand it by:
- being aware of the speaker's body language and what it means;
- being aware of the speaker's tone of voice – does it match what is being said, or is it perhaps ironic or sarcastic?
- concentrating on the most important points the speaker is making so that you can remember them and ask about them or reply to them later;
- noting any bias, contradictions or misuse of evidence that you can challenge;
- asking for something to be explained or justified in more detail.

The last point above is particularly important. It is a technique which, as long as you don't overdo it, both increases your understanding of the topic and shows that you are listening with interest.

Listening in a group

When you are listening to others in a group you should:
- ask questions which draw out other people's opinions;
- ask for explanation, or more detail of others' ideas;
- summarise what others have said to check that you understand them;
- show that you are interested and involved through your body language.

Showing listening through speaking

When it is your turn to speak, you can continue to show that you were listening with interest and understanding by:
- replying directly to the main points raised by previous speakers and adding to them with your own ideas and opinions;
- questioning any bias, wrong information, etc. which you think was given by presenting your own points of view;
- using what others have said in reaching your own conclusions and directly ask the rest of the group if they agree with you or not.

Active listening (1–2)

1 Name five significant aspects of body language which reveal how involved you are as a listener (5).

2 As a member of a discussion group, what four things can you do to encourage others to make useful contributions? (4)

3 Identify as many examples as you can of good listening skills shown in this extract from a group discussion.

(a) ANDY   No, but even so, I think nuclear power should be banned. (2)

(b) CLARE   So do I, but lots of people disagree. (1)

(c) HANIF   And do you know why? It's because it doesn't damage the environment the way that burning coal or oil does. (2)

(d) CLARE   But it's not as simple as that – if safety procedures at a nuclear power station fail, there won't be any environment left! (2)

(e) HANIF   That's a bit of an overstatement. (1)

(f) ANDY   No, I agree with Clare. Look at what happened at Chernobyl. Can't we agree that there are some dangers? (2)

(g) HANIF   I suppose so, but I don't think nuclear power should just be banned. (1)

1 Posture (1); facial expression (1); gestures and movements (1); eye-contact (1); arm position (1).

Remember that these are also important aspects of speaking – see question 2 under 'Check yourself' on page 111.

2 Ask questions which draw out other people's opinions (1); ask for explanation, clarification or more detail of others' ideas (1); summarise what others have said to check that you understand them (1); show that you are interested and involved through your body language (1).

These are ways that you can get involved in a discussion. You can gain marks for your speaking and listening skills even if you are not very interested in, or know much about, the subject.

3 (a) Andy replies to a previous speaker (1) and adds his own opinion (1).
  (b) Clare uses what Andy has said to express her own thoughts (1).
  (c) Hanif asks a question (1) and adds some evidence to support his own point of view (1).
  (d) Clare questions Hanif's evidence (1) and adds her own opinion (1).
  (e) Hanif questions what he sees as a biased view (1).
  (f) Andy adds some more evidence of his own (1) and then asks if the group can agree a conclusion (1).
  (g) Hanif replies to Andy's question (1).

TOTAL

Background information

The exam board will usually provide an introduction and/or brief notes which tell you something about the texts and their authors. Read this carefully, as it may:

- provide you with background information about the texts or authors which will help you understand them better;
- help you relate different texts to one another by theme, genre or culture;
- prepare you for the kinds of questions you may be asked in the examination.

Annotation

Most exam boards allow you to annotate pre-release material, so:

- write the meanings of any words or phrases which you are not sure of in the margin;
- underline or highlight words/phrases which you think may be good to refer to in your answers – perhaps because they are unusual or striking examples of imagery, characterisation, rhyme, etc.;
- devise your own symbols to cross-reference details from one text with another – perhaps if there are texts on a similar theme which use different approaches;
- note details of rhyme schemes and rhythms in poems, or the structure of stories if these are unusual or significant to their meaning;
- DO NOT write in lots of irrelevant background information – the examiner will want to see how you respond to the texts, not how much general knowledge you have;
- DO NOT write pre-prepared answers on the material – it is cheating, and may get you disqualified. In any case, you must answer the actual questions on the exam paper, not the ones you would like to answer.

Responding to the texts

Decide what you understand and like (or dislike) about each text. Think about different ways of reading them, so that you can write about alternative interpretations.

Make revision notes for yourself under these headings:
● text(s) I particularly enjoyed, and why
● text(s) I particularly disliked, and why
● thematic connections between texts
● interesting or unusual uses of language in texts
● interesting or unusual ideas in texts
● interesting or unusual writing techniques, devices or structures
● main points of interest in character, setting or theme
● similarities and differences between texts in relation to themes, ideas, techniques, purpose, audience, language, etc.

(DO NOT write them on the pre-release material itself, as this may get you disqualified.)

Even though you cannot put detailed notes on the actual pre-release material, you could devise a coding system and key which relates to the above list. It would be quite acceptable to write that onto the material and it might usefully jog your memory in the exam.

Finally...

REMEMBER to take your own annotated copy of the pre-release material into the exam BUT DON'T TAKE ANY OTHER NOTES!

Remember that you can only take your annotated pre-released material into the exam.

Before the exam
- Read Chief Examiners' reports on previous exams: these will tell you why answers succeed or fail generally, and the common mistakes candidates make.
- Study mark schemes published by your exam board: these will tell you how marks are gained in specific types of questions.
- Look at the kinds of questions you are likely to face by studying past papers: you will not then be surprised in the exam.
- Make sure that you know the latest syllabus requirements: again, this will prevent any nasty surprises in the exam.
- Practise writing to the time limits of the exam, ensuring that you can write neatly and accurately at speed.

Practise writing to the time limits of the exam.

In the exam
Read the instructions on the paper carefully. You should:
- establish **how many** questions you have to answer overall, whether some need to come from certain sections, whether there are choices within questions, etc.;
- work out **how long** to spend on each question. Apportion time to each question in relation to the marks it carries – in other words, spend twice as long on a question worth 10 marks than on one worth 5 marks.
- check **which text(s) or part(s) of text(s)** you need to use in answering reading questions;
- check whether writing questions require you to use your own **knowledge** and/or **imagination**, or whether there is some text you can use for ideas.

Reading questions

Read each **piece of text** carefully and make **brief notes** on:
- your first reactions to events/settings/characters in fiction texts;
- your first reactions to information/facts/opinions in non-fiction texts;
- any ideas/concerns/attitudes that strike you as interesting;
- initial thoughts about language/technique/presentation.

Read **each question** carefully so that you can:
- understand exactly what is required, looking at key words such as **How?** or **Why?** Underline key words so that you remember to address them in your answer.
- use any prompts to help you focus and structure your answer, remembering that they may be listed in order of difficulty;
- keep focused on the question. Refer to it in your answer, and ensure that all you write is relevant.

Planning answers

Plan your answer in note or outline form. This ensures that you:
- don't rush into writing your actual answer before you have got a good idea of what you want to say;
- decide on the overall structure of your answer, so that it is logical and coherent;
- decide which are the best textual references to use.

Checking

Check your final answer. Have you:
- expressed yourself clearly, with accurate spelling and punctuation?
- set out quotations clearly and accurately?
- included all the material you planned to use?
- ended with a firm conclusion which refers back to the question?

All types of writing

In any kind of writing under exam conditions make sure that you:

- understand how to use stimulus material if it is provided;
- make notes about content, bearing in mind the time available;
- make an outline paragraph plan to help you structure your material;
- consider drafting opening and closing paragraphs in some detail to ensure that they are effective;
- write at your normal speed, taking care over accuracy and legibility;
- constantly think about purpose and audience: are you presenting the right kind of material in the right kind of way?

Writing to explore, imagine, entertain

- Decide on the ideas, feelings and situations that you want to *explore* in your writing.
- *Imagine* the sort of behaviour, dialogue, reactions and settings that will make your characters believable.
- Remember that to *entertain* does not necessarily mean humour: suspense, surprise and conflict are all equally acceptable.

Writing to inform, explain, describe

- Think **purpose**. What is the point of the information, explanation or description you are writing?
- Think **audience**. How will age, gender, interest, need, etc. affect the tone and style of your writing?
- Think **response**. Do you want your reader to feel challenged, amused, reassured, flattered? Your choice of language needs to reflect this.

Writing to argue, persuade, instruct

- Think about the **viewpoint** you adopt. Is it to be a powerful one-sided statement or a rational consideration of different opinions?
- Think about the **language** you use. Will it achieve most by shocking readers, or by being cool and distanced?
- Think about the **evidence** you can use to support your case and affect the reader's response.

EXAMINATION HINTS (4)

Writing to analyse, review, comment

- Convey the special qualities of whatever you are writing about by **analysing** what effect it has on you, and why.
- Collect evidence. Weigh one aspect against another, so that you **review** the subject thoroughly.
- Summarise your thoughts and feelings through clearly expressed **comments**.

Avoiding common mistakes

Reading

- Comment, don't just describe – think *how* and *why* rather than *what*.
- Use quotation selectively, not just everything you can think of.
- Analyse specific details of language and presentation – don't make vague generalisations.

Writing

- Keep to the subject – don't twist a question to fit something you had prepared earlier.
- Keep narratives simple and explanations relevant and logical – don't try to be too clever.
- Make sure your tone is appropriate – don't ever forget the audience.

SCORE CHART (1)

Topic	Check yourself	Points out of 20
Reading prose fiction	1	
Reading prose fiction	2	
Reading poetry	3	
Reading poetry	4	
Reading drama	5	
Reading beneath the surface	6	
Comparing texts	7	
Settings	8	
Language and devices in fiction	9	
Structure in fiction texts	10	
Types of non-fiction texts	11	
Media texts	12	
Fact and opinion	13	
Following an argument	14	
Structure in non-fiction texts	15	
Presentational devices	16	
Language in non-fiction texts	17	
Spelling	18	
Punctuation	19	
Vocabulary and style	20	
Sentence structures	21	
Structuring whole texts	22	
Presenting written work	23	
Writing	24	
Writing	25	
Writing	26	
Writing	27	
Organising talk	28	
Active listening	29	

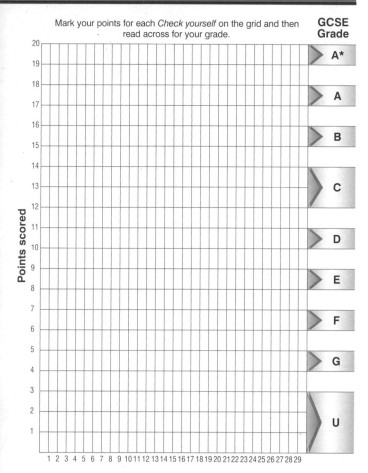

Mark your points for each *Check yourself* on the grid and then read across for your grade.

GCSE Grade

A*

A

B

C

D

E

F

G

U

Points scored

Check yourself